Test Bank to Accompany

Explorations
an Introduction to Astronomy

Introductory essay by
Dr. Arthur Young,
Professor of Astronomy
San Diego State University

Questions by
Dr. Arthur Young
and Thomas T. Arny,
Associate Professor of Physics and Astronomy
University of Massachusetts, Amherst

 Mosby

St. Louis Baltimore Berlin Boston Carlsbad Chicago London Madrid
Naples New York Philadelphia Sydney Tokyo Toronto

Copyright ©1994 by Mosby–Year Book, Inc.

All rights reserved. Except in classes in which *Explorations: an Introduction into Astronomy* is used, no part of this publication may be reproduced, stored in a retrieval system, or transmitted in any form or by any means, electronic, mechanical, photocopying, recording, or otherwise without prior written permission from the publisher.

Printed in the United States of America

Mosby–Year Book, Inc.
11830 Westline Industrial Drive
St. Louis, Missouri 63146

4694-4

Design Theory of Multiple-Choice Tests:
Introductory Astronomy

Dr. Arthur Young
Professor of Astronomy
San Diego State University

THE TYRANNY OF TESTING

In 1962, following a long series of articles in The American Scholar, Harper's Magazine, and Physics Today, the eminent physicist and scholar Banesh Hoffmann published a book with the title, "The Tyranny of Testing". In his typically cogent and forceful manner, Hoffmann set out in that monograph the entirety of his strong objections to the widespread use of the (objective) multiple choice form of testing and evaluation of human skills, knowledge, performance, and intellect. Anyone who has ever used such a method of testing, or who is contemplating such a venture, certainly should read Hoffmann's sublimely introspective analysis before proceeding any further into those treacherous waters.

Professor Hoffmann's positions are well documented and very well thought through and expressed. His thesis, in very broad overview, is that the multiple choice format does not actually test most of what its users purport to be testing, and often it puts the most able students at a disadvantage relative to their clever, but less able, peers. The scholarly and general condemnation of such testing by Hoffmann must be carefully examined, for if it is universally true, then such examinations should be banished (perhaps Baneshed) from the academic evaluation process. A somewhat more specific synopsis of Hoffmann's viewpoint is that multiple choice tests fail to test the depth of native human intelligence (whatever that really is) or of specific human aptitudes for such domains as science, mathematics, or writing. They fail especially to evaluate human creativity in any of its variegated forms. Even more mundane matters such as critical thinking, reading comprehension, and communication skills are tested only at a superficial level, placing the finest and deepest thinkers at a relative disadvantage. In a summarized form, these assertions are supported by noting the following facts about the multiple choice format.

1. The format denies creative thinkers any opportunity to demonstrate their originality.

2. Shrewd but superficial thinkers have a distinct advantage over deeper thinkers who often discover in

questions subtle ambiguities that were not noticed by the examiner.

3. The format denies the opportunity to elucidate the quality of thought that led to a correct answer (i.e. convoluted logic; penetrating analysis; or shrewd guessing).

4. The best prepared students often see deeper into questions than the examiner intended, and thus become confused when none of the choices seem to be correct, or more than one could be correct.

5. The format prevents the examiner from asking the most deep and searching questions that are possible.

6. Awkward grammar or a poor choice of a word or phrase can introduce unintended ambiguity into an otherwise reasonable question.

7. The format encourages and may even reward guessing.

8. Deep understanding (of concepts) cannot be tested and may even be lacking in those persons who score very well.

9. In cases where more than one answer could be equally correct, the student must attempt to probe the mind and the intent of the examiner rather than the subject.

Having such an array of faults, it is difficult to see that there are any redeeming qualities to multiple choice examinations.

Almost exclusively throughout his monograph, Hoffmann's criticisms are directed at the various products of the Educational Testing Service (E.T.S.) and the College Entrance Examination Board (C.E.E.B.) with special attention to the Scholastic Aptitude Test (S.A.T.) and the Graduate Record Examination (G.R.E.). Also among his targets are various I.Q. tests, the National Merit Scholarship Corporation, and various military and corporate testing for job aptitudes and promotions. Conspicuous by its absence is any direct critique of the use of multiple choice examinations for the evaluation of performance in specific courses, but there is little doubt of what Hoffmann's view of that would be.

A careful analysis of Hoffmann's critiques reveals that his analysis is both astute and largely correct. However, the fallacy of the testing methodology comes not from some inherent flaw in the multiple choice format, but rather in its indiscriminate use to test attributes for which it is clearly unsuited. Neither Hoffmann nor anyone else has offered a convincingly effective method for assessing native intelligence, scholastic (or other) aptitudes, or general intellectual achievement. A case might even be made that there is no effective way to quantify and measure such intangibles. Hoffmann's analysis leaves little doubt that the multiple choice examination format falls far short of achieving such goals, regardless of whether they are ultimately achievable or not.

In the discussion that follows, I maintain that the multiple choice format can be used effectively for the limited purpose of evaluation and certification of modest but measurable amounts of intellectual growth in sharply defined domains of knowledge.

In spite of differences in rhetoric among institutions, the basic goals of science courses in the liberal arts curriculum differ very little. Teaching methods, course contents, and styles differ more than do the basic objectives for such courses. In particular, there is no intention to teach science as if to a future professional, and thus there is no expectation that the amount of knowledge gained or the depth of its comprehension be commensurate with that of first year science students. Thus, there is no need for tests to evaluate depth of insights, problem solving competency, analytical skills, and originality since those are not among the goals of the courses.

The best courses strive to heighten the awareness of non-science students to the world of science and its values and methodology, while giving a greater appreciation for what science is about and what it has discovered about reality. High on the list of goals in all such courses is to impart some sense of critical thinking about scientific matters (and all else), and to elucidate the facts that lie at the foundations of contemporary knowledge and understanding of the universe. Some understanding of the great principles and laws that seem to define the structure of nature is central to all such courses.

Testing and evaluation is therefore directed at the assessment of growth in these broader domains, within the confines of the subject matter that comprises the course. The objective, multiple choice format is capable of providing such an assessment, but only if great care is taken in the creation of the questions. In particular, the overwhelming tendency for such questions to do no more than elicit useless memorized information must be avoided. It is possible, albeit challenging, to design multiple choice questions that probe for comprehension as well as knowledge, and for the limited ability to analyze and to apply knowledge that is expected of students who complete such courses.

The prevalent guide for the hierarchy of learning in contemporary education is Bloom's taxonomy which has the following six levels in order of increasing sophistication.

1. KNOWLEDGE: Information of fundamental importance, and the ability to recall it for appropriate situations. In astronomy this translates into knowing significant observational facts (e.g., the existence and properties of the cosmic background radiation), and fundamental laws such as those of Kepler.

2. COMPREHENSION: Understanding the meaning of knowledge and how it is obtained and justified. Following the previous example, this would imply an understanding of the interpretation of the cosmic background radiation and its implication for the structure of the universe; and an understanding of the implications of Kepler's laws upon the motions of orbiting objects and how those laws derive from the more general law of universal gravitation.

3. APPLICATION: Ability to use knowledge in new or unfamiliar situations. Recognition, for example, of how Kepler's laws can permit the determination of the mass of a planet would constitute a demonstration of this ability by

students in an introductory astronomy course.

4. ANALYSIS: An advanced form of application consisting of the ability to use knowledge to understand or to infer a new situation. Using Kepler's laws in a clever way to predict the orbital distance of an Earth satellite whose period is the same as that of the rotation of the earth, for example.

5. SYNTHESIS: Ability to combine two or more concepts or facts to infer yet another, or to achieve analysis. An example might be making assumptions about the structure of the Milky Way galaxy combined with Kepler's laws leading to an estimate of the number of stars in the Milky Way galaxy.

6. EVALUATION: Judgments based on critical thinking using acquired knowledge. The mature student evaluates the contemporary obsessions with astrology, the occult, the supernatural, and Creationism. A more subtle example is the ability to recognize the difference between a strongly suggestive argument, and one that is truly compelling. Evaluation is the most sublime form of critical thinking.

Distinctions between these categories are not always sharp, nor are they independent and mutually exclusive. The ability to apply knowledge presupposes ownership of the knowledge and reasonable comprehension of it as well. Analysis is a form of application, and synthesis usually involves some analysis. Good test questions will often combine more than one of the skills described by Bloom's taxonomy, while focusing upon one in particular. In the discussion of the examples, reference will be made wherever appropriate to particular categories in the taxonomy.

CRITICAL THINKING AND EVALUATION

Science is widely thought to epitomize rational and logical thinking, to the exclusion of the converse of those attributes. Such a parochial view of science overlooks the imaginative originality that is responsible for whatever could be called great about science. Nevertheless, students are often urged to learn some science in order to learn to think rationally and logically. One would hope that rational thinking is practiced universally in the academic community, so that a science course is not the sole exposure to such a virtue. Logic, a particular form of rational thinking, is better learned from logicians and mathematicians than from scientists who use it when it serves their purposes, and who abandon it when it does not. However, one particular attribute of rationality that scientists develop to a high degree is critical thinking. The habit and the skill of critical thinking is a direct outgrowth of the intellectual competition to find the correct interpretation for the array of clues that nature displays about its construction. Since more than one interpretation is almost invariably possible for any set of observed phenomena, the quest for validity will always involve a critical analysis of different ideas that are put forward by original thinkers. The training of a scientist acquaints him or her with the history of such critical thinking; and the practice of science exposes him or her to its use. The proposals and the findings of a working scientist are subjected to the (often exaggerated) critical review of his peers; and the working scientist finds himself to be a critical reviewer of his colleagues. Experienced scientists become masters of critical thinking almost inadvertently! Any scientist who finds himself to be the only scientist on a committee, panel, or jury will usually be shocked by the lack of almost elementary critical thinking displayed by the other members. It is therefore of paramount importance that critical thinking, and its highest form, evaluation, be central components of what we teach and what we test for in our introductory science courses. I list below some of the attributes which a skilled critical thinker must possess.

1. The ability to recognize the presence of unsubstantiated assumptions in an argument; especially when the assumptions are tacit or implicit, and not stated explicitly.

2. The ability to recognize ambiguities or alternatives in the interpretation of otherwise factual information.

3. Awareness of the potential for unknown or unavailable information to alter an impression or an interpretation (i.e., the tentativeness of all conclusions based entirely upon facts).

4. Recognition of fallacies in statistical reasoning

(inferencing) using valid statistical information.

5. Alertness to subtle selection effects in the acquisition of sampled data, and their effects upon conclusions.

6. Recognition of non sequiturs and other forms of convoluted logic (e.g., post hoc ergo propter hoc) in arguments.

7. Ability to distinguish between arguments that are weak, arguments that are strong (weaker alternatives are possible), and arguments that are compelling (all reasonable alternatives are eliminated).

Testing for critical thinking skills is difficult. The basic strategy is to present situations in which most or all of the choices are reasonable, but only one can stand the test of sharp critical thinking. These are often the most difficult questions on any test. Frequently, the history of science offers a rich field for generating such questions.

EXAMPLES

1. In his determination of the circumference of the earth, Eratosthenes made each of the following assumptions except one. Which one was NOT a necessary assumption?

    A. The shape of the earth is a sphere.
    B. The distance from Syene to Alexandria is known.
    C. The distance to the sun is much larger than the radius of the earth.
    D. The earth rotates on an axis.
    E. Light travels on straight lines.

2. All of the following are actually observed phenomena. Which one permits a <u>compelling</u> argument that the earth is shaped like a sphere?

    A. Ships vanish over a distant horizon.
    B. The sky appears to turn around us.
    C. The altitude of the north star increases as an observer travels northward.
    D. During a lunar eclipse, the earth's shadow appears to be circular.

E. All lunar eclipses show the earth's shadow to be circular.

The expected answers are: 1-D; 2-E

Evaluation is both the most sublime form of critical thinking and the most difficult to test. By evaluation we mean the use of critical thinking to exercise judgment, and often that must be subjective. A partial list of attributes for skilled evaluation is as follows.

1. Ability to distinguish between poor assumptions and good assumptions when making assumptions is unavoidable.

2. Ability to distinguish weak arguments from strong arguments.

3. Ability to asses likely vs. unlikely interpretations for factual information.

4. Ability to asses the reliability of factual information, considering such matters as measurement uncertainty and selection effects.

A touchstone of critical evaluation that can easily be tested in the multiple choice format is the ability to distinguish between model-dependent and model-independent information. An abbreviated example of such questioning is shown here.

EXAMPLE

Identify which of the following factual statements is model-dependent and which is model-independent using the following code:
$$A = \text{model-independent}$$
$$B = \text{model-dependent}$$

1. The inclination of the ecliptic to the celestial equator is 23.4419 degrees.

2. The sun takes 365.2422 days to move from the Vernal Equinox around the ecliptic and back to the Vernal Equinox.

3. The temperature at the center of the sun is 13,478,000 K.

4. All of the dinosaurs perished in a relatively short time which took place 65 million years ago.

5. In February 1987 a supernova explosion was observed in the southern sky. A newspaper report quoted an astronomer who said that the energy liberated by the explosion was about 250 billion times the luminous energy of our sun.

The desired answers are: 1-A; 2-A; 3-B; 4-B; 5-B.

CONSTRUCTION OF MULTIPLE CHOICE QUESTIONS

Professor Hoffmann's analysis casts doubt upon the presumed objectivity of multiple choice examinations, but their efficiency is beyond question. For professors with enormous sized classes, or many sections of smaller ones, the grading of examinations becomes a major consumer of time. For some, that may well be just part of the responsibility of teaching the course, but many others have other courses to teach and are engaged in research programs and other academic duties. An efficient testing method that does not sacrifice rigor is highly desirable.

Those who hold the opinion that only a written essay examination retains the desired rigor would do well to read Chapter 3 of professor Hoffmann's book before dismissing the multiple choice format a priori. There is a good reason why he did not choose to call his book, The Tyranny of Multiple Choice Testing! It is particularly ironic, if not entirely hypocritical, when faculty who eschew the use of multiple choice examinations for their own courses utilize S.A.T. and G.R.E test scores as virtually infallible indicators for entrance into their own programs!

Good examinations are teaching and learning experiences as well as tools for evaluation. By the particular questions that are asked, the instructor tacitly communicates which things are most important. By posing questions that require application, students discover how that is done since that is not a normal part of the studying process for non-science students. Even more significantly, questions that elicit application, analysis, and synthesis make the students aware of just how much growth they have achieved as a result of their passive assimilation of new knowledge. Many students, even those who attain high grade scores, do not appreciate the magnitude nor the significance of what they have learned unless they are pressed into using it by an examination that requires much more than rote responses.

In what follows, I give examples of questions that are designed to focus upon each one of the categories in Bloom's taxonomy, though not to the exclusion of all the other categories. I discuss the strategy of each question itself, and the general strategy for creating questions in that category. Although the test bank contains many questions that focus on all of the categories, instructors will want to augment them with some of their own that are tailored to the particular topics and issues that are emphasized in their own courses. By elucidating the strategies for doing that, I hope to make that process simpler and quicker than it is reputed to be. Following those discussions, I consider the theory of creating the foils; i.e., the incorrect responses in each question that accompany the correct one.

Unlike a first year course in physics or mathematics, our goal is not to test for a level of competency, or of potential for more advanced studies yet to come. We are testing instead for expanded awareness about the nature of science as an investigatory process; for comprehension of concepts about nature; for critical thinking; and for the foundations upon which knowledge is based. We are also testing to see if new knowledge has been acquired, and if old misconceptions have been eradicated. Using Bloom's taxonomy as an outline, I discuss the strategies for such testing under each of the categories.

KNOWLEDGE

In its broadest sense, science can be viewed as all of the activities and processes by means of which human beings journey from awareness to comprehension, concerning the phenomena of nature. Science begins with awareness of the existence of physical things, of their observable properties, and of physical occurrences or processes. Therefore, the body of knowledge contains an enormous amount of such empirical information, without interpretation. Comprehension comes from conceptualization, a uniquely human process. The body of knowledge then also contains models and theories that explain and interpret the empirical information and give meaning to those things about which we are aware.

For example, we (collectively) are aware that the earth experiences a regular and annual variation of seasons characterized by significant variations of the ambient temperature. For many students, that awareness is local, coming from their own personal experience. One form of expanded awareness comes from the disclosure that the same seasonal variations that we experience in the northern hemisphere are experienced in the southern hemisphere, but out of phase by one half year. An explanation for the seasonal variations will be connected to the behavior of the sun, but the hemispheric dichotomy eliminates variations of the distance as an explanation. The comprehension becomes deeper when other models are incorporated to explain why the sun behaves in the manner that causes the seasonal variations to occur. Testing for knowledge of this subject would center upon the empirical properties such as the hemispheric seasonal distinction, and the apparent motions of the sun at various critical latitudes like the equator, the arctic and antarctic circles, and the poles.

We (astronomers) are aware that a low level of microwave radiation is detected coming from all directions in the sky. We are aware of many of its properties such as its spectrum, and its nearly isotropic intensity, and its small departure from perfect isotropy. All of that is empirical knowledge, but because of its enormous significance it is appropriate that our students share that knowledge, and hence there will be test questions to insure that the existence and the principal properties of this radiation is known to them. However, it is equally important that the body of knowledge that we transmit, and for which we test, includes our sense for what is the importance of this radiation for understanding our universe, and what is our current explanation for its existence and its properties.

Knowledge, as we define it for the general education course in astronomy, has two components. There is an empirical component that consists of awareness of various things, of their observable properties, and of phenomena that occur. There is also a conceptual component that consists of knowing the contemporary explanations for such properties and phenomena, even if that does not include a deep and genuine understanding of those explanations. Under this category, we test for the knowledge of explanations, whereas we test for a deeper level of comprehension in succeeding categories. If the testing is constructed properly, the grade that is achieved represents some measure of the sophistication of learning rather than just the amount.

Information is a form of knowledge, often in a very compressed way, such as a single number. One set of examples is as follows.

1. The (approximate) diameter of our Milky Way galaxy.

2. The (approximate) number of stars in our Milky Way galaxy.

3. The (approximate) age of our sun.

4. The scale of the observable universe and the (approximate) distance to the most remote objects yet detected.

Yet another set of examples of information is the following.

1. The number of planets in our solar system.

2. The names of the planets and their order from the sun.

3. The seven principal spectral types of the stars.

4. The three principal types of galaxies.

The first set of factual information has real significance, having emerged from scientific inquiry, and it conveys some genuine knowledge about the universe in which we live. The second set consists of useless superficialities that do not have such significance. Names of things are assigned arbitrarily by people, and they typically contain no information about the entities themselves. Likewise, classes and types may seem scientific but they are merely arbitrary distinctions made by scientists, and they also contain little or no physical information of any particular importance.

Another useless form of knowledge that many textbooks burden students with is the arcane system of magnitudes for describing the apparent brightness of stars, and their relative luminosities. While it is very useful for an astronomer to know that a star with an absolute magnitude of 0.0 is nearly 100 times more luminous than our sun, and that one with an absolute magnitude of 6.0 is about one third as luminous as our sun, that is neither useful nor even reasonable for students who study astronomy as a general education science. Even for those very few students who know what logarithms are, and for the tiny fraction of them who have some facility with logarithms, the system of astronomical magnitudes poses a real challenge. Stellar luminosities should always be expressed as ratios in terms of the solar luminosity, eliminating the need to comprehend our esoteric system. The burden is always upon us to signal what is important to know, and what is not.

When we pose questions that ask for memorized information, we are informing the students of what we think is sufficiently important that it should be committed to memory by any person who considers himself to be well informed about our science. In that same vein, we must ask ourselves what we would want our students to remember from our course, five years from now, and on into the future. We should keep in mind that anything that makes a profound impression (such as the size of our galaxy, or the distance to the most remote objects) is more likely to be retained for a lifetime than something as meaningless as the scrambled order of the spectral types of the stars; and profound impressions are also more worthy of such retention. By keeping these simple aphorisms in mind, most of the trivial questions that typically inhabit multiple choice examinations will vanish.

Perhaps the most important kind of knowledge consists of those things or those phenomena that constitute evidence for particular beliefs or viewpoints that are currently held by the scientific community. Since educated persons do not customarily accept things on faith, the burden is upon us to show the evidence for our own beliefs. Therefore, the most sophisticated kind of (memorized) knowledge is that which constitutes evidence for very important concepts and viewpoints, such as for evolution, or for the expansion of the universe. An important subset of that knowledge is empirical tests that are critical tests which discriminate between competing theories or viewpoints.

In summary, there are five domains of knowledge that are sufficiently important as to be tested for explicitly in examinations. These domains are:

1. Important phenomena or properties of nature.

2. Contemporary explanations for those phenomena or properties.

3. Significant information about natural structures.

4. Evidence upon which contemporary viewpoints are based.

5. Critical (observational) tests that distinguish between competing explanations for the same phenomena.

Each of the following sample questions illustrates the testing of one or more of those domains.

1. One month from now, a constellation of stars that we see nearly overhead at 9:00 P.M. tonight will be seen at 9:00 P.M. to be

      A. nearly overhead.
      B. lower in the western sky.
      C. lower in the eastern sky.
      D. lower in the southern sky.
      E. already set below the western horizon.

2. The patterns or constellations of stars seen in each of our seasons are different. That fact demonstrates that

    A. the earth must rotate upon an axis.
    B. the earth must revolve on an orbit around the sun.
    C. the earth must be a sphere.
    D. the sun must move relative to the stars.
    E. there must be parallax angles for the stars.

3. The night sky is very dark. The currently accepted explanation for that observed fact is that

    A. the sun is below the horizon.
    B. the universe is not infinitely large.
    C. the universe is expanding.
    D. the universe is evolving.
    E. the universe is not infinitely old.

4. How does the age of the oldest stars that astronomers have ever found compare to the age of the oldest rocks that geologists have ever found?

    A. The oldest stars are about twice the age of the oldest rocks.
    B. The oldest stars are 10 times older than the oldest rocks.
    C. The oldest stars and the oldest rocks are about the same age.
    D. Astronomers cannot determine the age of the oldest stars.
    E. Geologists cannot determine the age of the oldest rocks.

5. Astronomers are convinced that the sun is evolving. What is the <u>observed</u> evidence for that conviction?

    A. Changes actually observed on the surface of the sun.
    B. Ancient records show the sun was different long ago.
    C. The mass of the sun is observed to be decreasing.
    D. The sun radiates energy that is not being replaced.
    E. 25% of the mass of the sun is helium.

6. The "red-shifts" of the spectra of distant galaxies constitute evidence that

   A. the universe is becoming cooler.
   B. the universe is expanding.
   C. the universe is evolving.
   D. the universe is in steady state.
   E. the galaxies are getting bigger.

7. Direct observational evidence that the scale of the universe is expanding comes from

   A. the cosmic background radiation.
   B. the darkness of the night sky.
   C. the "red-shifts" of the spectra of galaxies.
   D. the existence of quasars.
   E. the clustering of galaxies.

8. Each of the following statements is correct, but only one constitutes <u>evidence</u> that evolution has occurred in the universe. Which statement is evidence for evolution?

   A. Very distant galaxies appear smaller than nearby galaxies.
   B. Very distant galaxies appear dimmer than nearby galaxies.
   C. Ellipsoidal galaxies contain no free dust and gas.
   D. All quasars are very far away.
   E. There are more ellipsoidal galaxies than spiral galaxies.

9. A <u>critical test</u> that demonstrates that the earth rotates upon an axis is

   A. change of direction of a free swinging pendulum.
   B. the moving shadow on a sundial.
   C. the parallax of the stars.
   D. eclipses of the moon.
   E. only one hemisphere of the moon is ever seen from the earth.

The intended answers are:

1-B; 2-D; 3-E; 4-A; 5-D; 6-B; 7-C; 8-D; 9-A

Question (1) tests for rudimentary knowledge about the behavior of the sky. It would have been a ridiculous question to ask in ancient Athens since everyone with eyes knew how the sky behaves, even if not why it does so. In our modern technological age, very few people ever look directly at nature, and the motion of the sky is a surprise to most of our students and visitors to the observatory. The foils are crafted so that the better students will either select the correct answer at once, or ponder between choices B and C. Choices A and E implicitly quantify the phenomenon, and students who have actually looked at the sky will eliminate them at once. More capable students will recognize that one month generates about 30 degrees of sky displacement, and will thus eliminate those choices also. A student who selects choice D reveals a more serious academic problem.

Question (2) inverts the process, stating the observed behavior, and asking for its unambiguous meaning. Even some of the better students slip and select choice B, the commonly accepted explanation for the phenomenon that is described. The wording is careful and unambiguous; if that observed behavior could be understood only by orbital motion of the earth, the geocentric astronomy of the ancients would never have been conceived. Although I classify this as a KNOWLEDGE question, some critical thinking is needed to distinguish the subtle difference between choices B and D.

Question (3) is very esoteric, and one would expect that it can be answered successfully only by persons who have taken a modern course in astronomy. A student who answers it correctly might not understand the subtle reasoning that makes choice E the only correct response. Banesh Hoffmann might criticize the question for that weakness, but it was never intended to test that deeply. It tests for esoteric knowledge; not for esoteric comprehension. There are many variations on the phrasing of the question so that it can be used with slightly different nuance on different examinations. For example:

3. The darkness of the night sky is taken by modern astronomers to be evidence that

(same selection of responses)

3. Astronomers are now convinced that the universe is not infinitely old. Which of the following observed properties of the universe is evidence for that conviction?

    A. The "red-shifts" of the spectra of distant galaxies.
    B. Galaxies exist in clusters.
*C. The night sky is very dark.
    D. Most of the mass of the universe is hydrogen.
    E. Our sun is still on the main sequence.

Question (4) is intended to inform the students who memorized the age of the oldest known stars, that such information is more meaningful when it can be put into a broader context.

Although question (5) is categorized as a KNOWLEDGE question, the selection of response D requires some comprehension of what is actually meant by evolution. A student who selects response D may not know the intricate details of the prognosis for solar evolution, but demonstrates instead a mature realization of what evolution means, and what conditions insure that it must occur. It is far more likely, and certainly more valuable, that such an insight will be retained long after the complex details of solar interior evolution have faded from memory.

Questions (6) and (7) are two versions of the same question with a different twist. They are not intended to be used on the same examination. There is a conceptual symmetry between knowing what evidence supports a particular viewpoint (question 7), and what viewpoint is supported by a particular piece of evidence (question 6). Students in a general education science course should become adept at both of those versions.

Question (8) is a somewhat more subtle variance of the idea that is tested by question (5). Once students recognize that evolution of any physical system is characterized by irreversible change, then evidence for evolution is going to be found either in a record of the past that can be compared with the present, or in some process that cannot reverse. Question (5) tested for a recognition of the latter, and question (8) tests for a recognition of the former.

Although I classify question (8) as one for KNOWLEDGE, it requires some synthesis as well. The students should know that quasars have unique physical properties that differ markedly from ordinary galaxies (even if they do not recall exactly what those differences are). The more astute students should recognize that "far away" translates into "long ago". Putting these ideas together (synthesis) means that the absence of nearby quasars is a signal from the universe that it was once different from the way it is now; the signature of evolution.

Choices C, D, and E in question (9) are all critical tests, but for concepts other than the rotation of the earth. The student who mindlessly memorizes all things in the course notes that were ever called "critical tests", finds himself confronted with four of them, when only one is the right one for this circumstance.

COMPREHENSION

Those who teach elementary science courses usually place a greater emphasis upon COMPREHENSION than on any of the other categories of Bloom's taxonomy. The reason for that is the fact that knowledge without understanding is of little use, and the more sophisticated attributes of application and analysis generally require more mathematical training and more advanced scientific course-work. The distinctions between comprehension, application, and analysis are not at all sharp, and the overlap is considerable. Nevertheless, it is possible to sort them out in the testing arena, though never exclusively. The principal strategy to test for COMPREHENSION of concepts is to require the student to provide an explanation for why something happens the way it does. Needless to say, comprehension is not demonstrated if it is possible to remember an explanation given in a textbook or a class discussion. Therefore, it is necessary to confront the student with unfamiliar situations which can be explained in terms of concepts that are supposedly comprehended.

COMPREHENSION (of concepts, models, or laws) can also be demonstrated by correctly associating a phenomenon with a physical law or with a specific model that explains it, with the caveat that it not be possible to have memorized that association. A variation that permits use of mathematics is to correctly associate a phenomenon with an equation which expresses the idea that explains the phenomenon. The latter can be done either by embedding the equation in the choices along with other, irrelevant equations, or by providing a list of equations with the examination and requesting that the appropriate one be selected. The latter technique has the additional advantage of discouraging students from memorizing equations since they know that all of them will be listed on the examination, and encouraging them to focus upon the meaning of the equations.

The following examples show all of these strategies.

1. When you switch off the lights in your room at night, the walls, the ceiling, and the floor are at a temperature of 300 K. Why are you not dazzled by the radiation that they emit?

> A. Because they do not emit any radiation.
> B. Because they are not anything like black bodies.
> C. Nothing can radiate below a temperature of 3000K.
> D. Human eyes cannot see infrared radiation.
> E. Human eyes cannot see ultraviolet radiation.

2. The absorption lines of calcium in the spectrum of our sun's atmosphere are much darker than those of hydrogen. The explanation for this is that

> A. the sun is a very unusual star.
> B. there is more calcium than hydrogen in the sun.
> C. most of the hydrogen is ionized.
> D. the hydrogen has been converted to helium.
> E. most of the hydrogen is in the ground state.

3. The shadow of a flagpole in sunlight does not appear to have a sharp edge (boundary). The reason for that is

> A. light does not travel on exactly straight lines.
> B. the earth's atmosphere refracts the light.
> C. the sun is not a point source of light.
> D. scattering by the earth's atmosphere diffuses it.
> E. flagpoles are round and thus have no sharp edge.

4. Pushing a shopping cart is much easier to do than pushing an automobile. Write the letter corresponding to the equation on the back page that expresses this fact.

> NOTE: Five equations are printed on the back page; one of them is $F = ma$

5. Halley's comet orbits the sun on a very elliptical orbit with a period of 75 years. When it was near the sun in 1985 it spent only 5 months there. That is a direct consequence of

> A. Kepler's I law.
> B. Kepler's II law.
> C. Kepler's III law.
> D. the basic property of all conic sections.
> E. perturbations by the inner planets.

6. Which one of the following statistical samples could be considered to be 100% complete?

> A. The 1049 stars known to be within 20 parsecs.
> B. The 9110 brightest known stars in the sky.
> C. The 5367 known clusters in the milky way.
> D. The 20 fastest known (radial velocity) stars.
> E. No sample could ever be 100% complete.

The intended answers are: 1-D; 2-E; 3-C; 4-($F = ma$); 5-B; 6-B

Since black-body radiation is typically discussed in the context of stellar photospheres, question (1) probes for a comprehension of the general properties in a familiar local situation, but very different from stars. If Wien's law is understood, then it will be apparent that cool objects must radiate primarily in the far infrared.

Question (2) probes the understanding of the Saha-Boltzmann explanation of atomic spectra. Some specific knowledge is needed to answer both of those questions, but that is not an unreasonable expectation.

Question (3) is more difficult, requiring some analytical thought. Since bright point sources of light are not commonly found in daily life, students cannot appeal to experience for an answer. Many students have probably never noticed that shadows rarely have sharp edges!

Question (4) may actually help students to put Newton's second law into context, recognizing that the difficulty of pushing something is just a measure of how much force is needed to achieve a given acceleration.

Kepler's II law is generally discussed in terms of its effect on the speed of a planet moving on an orbit. Question (5) puts the law into the less familiar context of the time required to move over an arc of an ellipse.

Question (6) is the most challenging since it requires not only comprehension of the concept of statistical completeness and incompleteness, but also some knowledge of how such things as the nearest stars are located, and why selection effects disturb surveys like that.

APPLICATION

An elementary course in astronomy is usually not sufficient to permit much APPLICATION of the concepts that are learned and even comprehended. However, a rudimentary form of application can be achieved by means of a few strategies. One strategy makes use of slides or overhead transparencies projected during the examination, with the questions directed at each one. A modicum of coordination is required to carry this out within the limitations of time that usually prevail. There is an almost irresistible temptation to use this format for identification of types of objects like globular clusters, planetary nebulae, etc. and that is a legitimate use of this format under the category of KNOWLEDGE.

However, it takes on the category of APPLICATION if, for example, stellar spectra are projected and the question asks to identify which star is the hottest; which the coolest; which is a binary; which is the fastest; etc.

Light curves of eclipsing binaries can provide more applications by asking which one has only partial eclipses; which one has two stars with nearly the same temperature;

which one has two stars with the biggest difference of surface temperature; which one probably has the shortest orbital period (or which one shows evidence of significant tides); etc.

Color-magnitude diagrams for clusters provide a format for asking which cluster is the youngest; which is the oldest; etc.

Application of the Stefan-Boltzmann law of black-body radiation can be had by constructing an idealized H-R diagram with stars located at temperature coordinates of 3000K, 6000K, and 12000K along the main sequence, and designated as (A), (B), and (C) respectively. The luminosities of these stars are 10^{-2}, 1, 10^3 respectively, in units of the solar luminosity. Star (D) is then located at a temperature coordinate of 3000K, with a luminosity of 10^2 in solar units (simulating a cool giant), and star (E) is placed at temperature coordinate 12000K with a luminosity of 10^{-2} in solar units (simulating a white dwarf). The line of questioning can then proceed as follows.

1. By what factor is the radius of star (D) larger than that of star (A)?

      A. 10
      B. 100
      C. 1000
      D. 3
      E. 30

2. By what factor is the radius of star (D) larger than that of star (B)?

      A. 10
      B. 20
      C. 40
      D. 100
      E. Not possible to compute from information given.

3. Identify the star that must have the largest radius.

The intended answers are: 1-B; 2-C; 3-D.

By making the arithmetic trivially simple, the questions probe the ability to apply the black-body law to stars, using nothing but scaling relations. The more able students recognize that question (3) is a contest between stars (C) and (D). Since the surface temperature of star (C) is 4 times larger than that of star (D), its surface radiates 256 times as much energy per unit area. If the two stars were of the same radius, that would be the ratio of their luminosities. Since the actual ratio is just a factor of 10, star (D) must have a larger radius than star (C) (specifically about 5 times larger). Clearly, question (3) crosses from pure APPLICATION to some ANALYSIS. Other variations of this question can be made by substituting 9000K, 15000K, or 30000K for 12000K and by taking some liberties with the luminosities, permitting other combinations of stars to be compared.

Another strategy for APPLICATION is to present an actual model for something like the interior of the sun or of a star, or for the structure and dynamics of the Milky Way galaxy, etc. The line of questioning then involves a direct interpretation of the model. The following is an example using a solar interior model.

Fraction of the Radius	Temperature (K)	Fraction of the Mass	Fraction of the Luminosity
0.00	15,500,000	0.000	0.000
0.04	15,000,000	0.008	0.080
0.10	13,000,000	0.070	0.420
0.20	9,500,000	0.350	0.950
0.30	6,700,000	0.640	0.998
0.40	4,800,000	0.850	1.000
0.50	3,400,000	0.940	1.000
0.60	2,200,000	0.982	1.000
0.70	1,200,000	0.994	1.000
0.80	700,000	0.998	1.000
0.90	310,000	0.999	1.000
1.00	6,000	1.000	1.000

1. Which of the columns lists actual measured data?

    A. Fraction of the radius.
    B. Temperature.
    C. Fraction of the mass.
    D. Fraction of the luminosity.
    E. None.

2. What fraction of the mass of the sun generates 95% of the luminosity of the sun?

    A. 5%
    B. 15%
    C. 25%
    D. 35%
    E. 50%

3. Approximately what fraction of the VOLUME of the sun generates 95% of the solar luminosity?

    A. 1%
    B. 5%
    C. 10%
    D. 20%
    E. 30%

4. Approximately how much more dense is the central core of the sun (innermost 4%) than is the entire sun as a whole?

    A. 8 times.
    B. 50 times.
    C. 125 times.
    D. 500 times.
    E. 1000 times.

5. At what temperature inside the sun does the model indicate that ALL thermonuclear fusion of hydrogen into helium has stopped occurring?

    A. 15,000,000 K
    B. 13,000,000 K
    C. 9,500,000 K
    D. 6,700,000 K
    E. 4,800,000 K

6. At approximately what fraction of the radius of the sun is the temperature GRADIENT largest?

    A. 0.02
    B. 0.07
    C. 0.15
    D. 0.25
    E. 0.35

The intended answers are: 1-E; 2-D; 3-A; 4-C; 5-E; 6-C.

Question (2) requires no more than the ability to interpret the actual meaning of the tabular values (i.e., read the table properly).

Question (3) requires some simple calculation and knowledge of how volume depends on radius for a sphere.

Question (4) may be the most difficult for non-mathematical students. A calculator might be helpful to insure correct arithmetic, but the real challenge is to decide how to utilize the numbers in the table (i.e., APPLICATION).

Question (5) is a particularly good example of APPLICATION of knowledge since it asks for something that is not explicitly tabulated.

Question (6) is also a good example of APPLICATION since it requires that the student understands exactly what is meant by a temperature "gradient", and how that manifests inside a star. Again, a calculator would help to eliminate mistakes in arithmetic.

One of the most charming strategies for testing APPLICATION is to simulate a "Walk Under the Night Sky", whereby the student taking the examination is to imagine that he or she is walking with a friend at night, and the friend asks probing questions about what is actually seen. This is as much a learning experience as a testing experience since the student must connect abstract astronomical knowledge with things that can be seen directly with human eyes. It is also directed at playing down the importance of knowing names of stars and of constellation patterns, and substituting meaningful physical knowledge instead. I often suggest to students that they might prepare for this part of the examination by actually taking a friend (not a member of the class) for such a walk, and responding to his or her questions. I caution them that their friend will undoubtedly ask questions that are far more difficult than any that I would ask them!

A WALK UNDER THE NIGHT SKY

Now that you have completed a course in modern astronomy you could take a friend outside on some clear, dark night and explain to him (or her) some remarkable things about what is actually seen. For example, you could point out that stars have different colors and show your friend an example of an orange colored star and a blue colored star (even though you do not know their names).

1. You would tell your friend that the different colors are caused by

   A. different chemical compositions.
   B. Doppler shifts caused by their motions.
   C. different surface temperatures.
   D. different luminosities.
   E. absorption by interstellar dust.

2. You would then point out that the orange colored stars must be

   A. the coolest ones.
   B. the hottest ones.
   C. the most luminous ones.
   D. least luminous ones.
   E. the smallest ones.

3. Your friend asks how you can tell which objects are stars and which are planets. You reply that it is not apparent from just looking, but planets reveal themselves by

   A. changing color each night.
   B. changing position among the stars each night.
   C. changing brightness each night.
   D. setting after the sun in the west each night.

        E. rising before the sun in the east each morning.

4. Your friend asks if the stars shine by reflecting sunlight, like our moon does. You reply that they emit light of their own, and we know that because

        A. stars appear to have different colors.
        B. stars have different absorption line spectra.
        C. stars twinkle, but the sun gives steady light.
        D. stars are not large enough to reflect any light.
        E. the sun does not shine at night.

5. "Are the brightest stars the ones that are closest to us?", your friend asks, and you reply that they are not necessarily the closest because

        A. brightness is not related to distance.
        B. big stars always appear brighter than small
        C. hot stars always appear brighter than cool stars.
        D. binaries emit twice as much light as single stars
        E. luminosities differ by more than brightness.

6. "Of all the stars we can see in the sky tonight, which is the largest one?", your friend asks. You search all over the sky and then point to one that is

        A. bright and orange.
        B. bright and blue.
        C. twinkling most rapidly.
        D. brighter than all other visible stars.
        E. moving faster than the other stars.

7. Your friend asks if the stars will shine forever, and you tell him (her) that every star must die someday because

        A. eventually everything must die.
        B. all hot things eventually cool down.
        C. stars consume a finite supply of hydrogen fuel.
        D. the universe is expanding.
        E. they fall into a black hole in the center of our
           milky way galaxy.

8. "What happens to stars when they die?", your friend asks, and you reply that most of them become

   A. black holes.
   B. brown dwarfs.
   C. red dwarfs.
   D. white dwarfs.
   E. neutron stars.

9. "Can we see any dead stars in the sky tonight?", your friend asks, and you reply that none are visible because

   A. no stars have died yet in our galaxy.
   B. dead stars do not radiate any light.
   C. it is impossible to tell which ones are dead.
   D. dead stars are only found in clusters.
   E. dead stars have very low luminosity.

10. You then show your friend that we are inside a great stellar system shaped like a disk, by pointing out

    A. the line of the ecliptic.
    B. the bright blue stars.
    C. the horizon.
    D. the milky way.
    E. the north star.

11. Your friend then asks, "if all the stars are in the galactic disk, then why do we see most of them all around us, far from the milky way?". You think for a moment until you realize that this is evidence that

    A. most stars are not really in our galaxy.
    B. most visible stars must be very near to us.
    C. interstellar dust must all be very far from us.
    D. the sun is located in an unusual place.
    E. we are very near the center of our own galaxy.

12. "If the universe is expanding, are all the stars in the night sky getting farther away from us?", your friend asks. You inform him (her) that such a notion is incorrect because

        A. only the remote regions of the universe expand.
        B. stars are very tightly bound to each other.
        C. our sun prevents the nearby stars from expanding.
        D. the expansion of the universe has stopped by now.
        E. it is the scale of spacetime that is expanding.

13. Your friend asks if the universe will ever stop expanding, and you reply that

        A. all things that expand must eventually contract.
        B. it cannot possibly ever stop expanding.
        C. astronomers do not yet know the answer to that.
        D. it will never be possible to know that.
        E. "God made Hell for people who ask that question."
                (a quote from St. Augustine)

The intended answers are: 1-C; 2-A; 3-B; 4-B; 5-E; 6-A; 7-C; 8-D; 9-E; 10-D; 11-B; 12-E; 13-C.

As you walk home at the end of a delightful evening of star gazing, your friend asks you the name of a bright orange colored star that is nearly overhead. You do not know its name, or even if it has one; but you recognize that it must be a very distant, evolved red giant. You have come to know the stars in a more meaningful way than by the arbitrary names given to them by some people who lived long ago and who knew nothing about what the stars really are.

ANALYSIS

We have treated APPLICATION as an ability to utilize knowledge and comprehension to account for real situations, and to recognize things in context. ANALYSIS is a more sophisticated version of application, requiring that knowledge and comprehension be used to deduce the circumstances of an unfamiliar situation. If COMPREHENSION is the hallmark of good elementary science courses, then ANALYSIS is the central theme of advanced courses. In such courses ANALYSIS is taught and tested for by means of contrived problems. A similar strategy can be used in the

General Education science course, albeit with decreased emphasis upon the use of formal mathematical operations. It is not inappropriate, however, to expect students in such courses to be able to carry through the arithmetic associated with the use of scaling laws. The following questions are designed to elucidate analytical thought in both qualitative and quantitative motifs.

1. If a simple convex lens has a focal length of 10 cm when it is illuminated with RED light, then its focal length when illuminated with BLUE light will be

       A. somewhat shorter than 10 cm.
       B. somewhat longer than 10 cm.
       C. precisely 10 cm.
       D. blue light cannot be brought to a focus.
       E. impossible to make such a prediction.

2. If a simple convex lens were immersed into a tank of water, its focal length in any color would

       A. remain unchanged.
       B. become much longer.
       C. become much shorter.
       D. not be measurable under water.
       E. no longer exist (cannot focus light under water).

3. Two proposals are put to NASA by two scientists in competition for limited funds. The proposals are:

       A. Send a probe directly into the sun (it will be destroyed, but it will relay valuable data for most of the voyage).
       B. Send a probe out of the solar system, directed to reach the nearest star, Alpha Centauri.

NASA decides to fund the least expensive mission. Based upon your knowledge of the physics of orbits, advise NASA which mission is cheaper (i.e., requires the least amount of energy).

4. Suppose that the eccentricity of the orbit of our moon were 0.8 instead of its actual value. How much larger would it appear to us when it was at perigee, than at apogee?

   A. 9 times larger.
   B. 1.8 times larger.
   C. 2.8 times larger.
   D. 4 times larger.
   E. It would appear the same size.

5. An artificial satellite of the earth in a circular orbit just above our atmosphere must move at about 18,000 mi/hr. Saturn has about 100 times the mass of the earth, and 9 times the radius of the earth. How fast must an artificial satellite move to be in a circular orbit just above Saturn's atmosphere?

   A. 42,000 mi/hr.
   B. 60,000 mi/hr.
   C. 36,000 mi/hr.
   D. 18,000 mi/hr.
   E. 9,000 mi/hr.

6. Astronauts working on a permanent base on the moon would notice that the earth

   A. rises in the east and sets in the west.
   B. rises in the west and sets in the east.
   C. never rises, sets, or moves.
   D. is above the horizon only for 2 weeks each month.
   E. rises and sets once each sidereal lunar month.

7. If, instead of the earth, the sun had a binary companion star in our orbit with the same mass as the sun, the orbital period of that binary would be

   A. 2 years.
   B. 1.4 years.
   C. 0.7 years.
   D. 0.5 years.
   E. 1 year (same as the earth's current period).

8. The orbital velocity of the earth is about 30 km/sec, and the velocity of light is nearly 300,000 km/sec. Our motion causes the wavelength of hydrogen-alpha photons (6563 A) from stars on the ecliptic to change by about

    A. 1.5 A.
    B. 3.5 A.
    C. 0.6 A.
    D. 0.3 A.
    E. 0.1 A.

9. The sun is like a black body radiating at a temperature of about 6000 K. The brightest wavelength that the sun emits is about 5000 A. What is the brightest emitted wavelength from a star whose temperature is 30,000 K?

    A. 100 A.
    B. 300 A.
    C. 500 A.
    D. 1000 A.
    E. 3000 A.

The intended answers are: 1-A; 2-B; 3-B; 4-A; 5-B; 6-C; 7-C; 8-C; 9-D.

Questions (1) and (2) require some analytical thinking without any mathematical structure. Question (2) is far the more difficult, testing the comprehension of refraction as depending upon the ratio of the indices of the two media, and how lenses focus light.

Question (3) requires knowing that the escape velocity is the square root of 2 times larger than the circular velocity. It tests analytical skill to recognize that the earth has the circular velocity, so it is necessary to remove 100% of that to send a probe to the sun, but only to increase it by about 41% to leave the solar system.
Question (4) requires knowing the definition of the eccentricity of an ellipse, and then a geometrical analysis to find the ratio of the distances of the two extremes from a single focus.

Question (5) requires that the equation for the circular velocity be known, but I provide such equations on a supplementary sheet to discourage memorization and encourage comprehension. This question is designed to give an appreciation for the use of such equations as scaling laws.

Question (6) tests the ability to use knowledge in a new way. Students should know that the moon rotates synchronously with its sidereal period, keeping one hemisphere facing us. It takes some imagination to see that the earth is therefore a synchronous satellite from the point of view of an observer on the moon.

Question (7) requires that Kepler's III law be used as a scaling law, but including the dependence upon mass that Kepler himself did not realize.

Question (8) is a straightforward application of the Doppler equation.

Question (9) requires that Wien's radiation law be treated as a scaling law.

SYNTHESIS

The taxonomic class that we designate as APPLICATION involves the utilization of KNOWLEDGE and COMPREHENSION to provide explanations; and the class called ANALYSIS is the more sophisticated version of application in which predictions are made about unfamiliar circumstances by making use of knowledge and comprehension. By the taxonomic class called SYNTHESIS we mean either of the previous two classes (APPLICATION; ANALYSIS) in which two or more different concepts must be put together to achieve the desired result of explanation or of prediction. This kind of thinking can be challenging to even the most adroit students since they are generally taught to think in serial fashion. Thus, a good examination in a general education science course should not contain very many questions of this type, since they test for skills that are not usually present in most of the students. It is unreasonable to expect that this level of sophisticated thinking can result from the brief and superficial treatment of science that most general education courses are obliged to provide. However, it is precisely questions of this type that provide the discrimination for the highest grades achieved on any one examination.

The strategy for creating questions that require SYNTHESIS is exactly the same as that for APPLICATION and ANALYSIS, with the exception that two different concepts are superimposed into the same situation. One very good way to achieve this is to consider how various phenomena would appear as observed from places other than our normal vantage point on the earth, or in the galaxy. Some of the following examples make use of that strategy.

1. The retrograde motion of Mars occurs at intervals of

       A. one Martian synodic period.
       B. one Martian sidereal period.
       C. one Earth year.
       D. one Earth month.
       E. unpredictable duration.

2. An observer on Mars (1.5 A.U. from the sun) would find the parallax of the nearest star to be

       A. 50% larger than it is measured from Earth.
       B. 50% smaller than it is measured from Earth.
       C. the same as it is measured from Earth.
       D. unmeasurable.
       E. variable.

3. Astronomers on Earth find that the distance to the nearest star (alpha Centauri) is 1.30 parsecs. If there were astronomers on Jupiter (5 A.U. from the sun) they would find the distance to this star to be

       A. 1.30 parsecs.
       B. 6.50 parsecs.
       C. 0.26 parsecs.
       D. 13.0 parsecs.
       E. 0.13 parsecs.

4. An astronomer on Mars (1.5 A.U. from the sun) would find that the effect of stellar aberration there is

    A. non-existent.
    B. larger than it is measured from Earth.
    C. the same as it is measured from Earth.
    D. smaller than it is measured from Earth.
    E. reversed from the way it appears from Earth.

5. The earth orbits the sun with a velocity of about 30 km/sec. The velocity of light is about 300,000 km/sec. Astronomers who observe the 3 K cosmic background radiation in the direction of the orbital motion of the earth will find it to be

    A. cooler by 0.0003 K.
    B. hotter by 0.0003 K.
    C. cooler by 0.0001 K.
    D. hotter by 0.0001 K.
    E. unchanged since it comes from the universe.

6. Voyager pictures showed that the Great Red Spot on Jupiter rotates counterclockwise. Since the spot is in the southern hemisphere of Jupiter, this observation shows that

    A. material is flowing into the Great Red Spot.
    B. material is flowing out of the Great Red Spot.
    C. material in the spot does not flow in or out.
    D. the Great Red Spot must be turbulent.
    E. the Great Red Spot must be a solid object.

The intended answers are: 1-A; 2-A; 3-C; 4-D; 5-B; 6-B.

Question (1) links the explanation for retrograde motion with the concept of the synodic period.

Question (2) probes the concept of parallax in a broader context, illustrating its generality, and that it is not a phenomenon of the earth. The student must connect the concept of parallax and that of distance, recognizing that although the distance to the nearest star is the same from Mars as it is from Earth, the parallax is not the same since it is a relative measurement (i.e. the ratio of the distance of the planet from the sun to the distance of the star from the sun). The question can be made more difficult by asking about the proper motion of a star. In an absolute sense, the angular velocity of a star seen from Mars is the same as when it is seen from Earth. However, since proper motion is expressed as arc seconds per year, it will be found to be smaller by an observer on Mars because the year is longer.

Question (3) addresses this issue more directly, requiring the student to recognize that the parsec is a relative unit of distance, and not an absolute unit. Since the orbit of Jupiter is 5 times larger than the orbit of the earth, the (Jupiter) parsec is 5 times larger than that defined by the orbit of the earth. Thus the distance to the nearest star is a smaller number of (Jupiter) parsecs. Greater emphasis on SYNTHESIS can be had with this question by stating it in terms of distance measured in light-years. The distance to the nearest star is about 4 light-years as measured from the earth. However, as a consequence of Kepler's III law, the year for Jupiter is longer than the year for the earth. Since the velocity of light is an absolute constant, the distance to the nearest star in (Jupiter) light-years is smaller than from the earth by just the ratio of the orbital periods of the two planets. Since the size of the orbit of Jupiter is specified in the question, the student is expected to use Kepler's III law to estimate the orbital period. Jupiter's orbital period is nearly 12 years, so the distance to the nearest star would appear from Jupiter to be about 1/3 of a light-year.

Question (4) is a classic example of SYNTHESIS in which the phenomenon of aberration is linked with the physics of orbital motion. The student must recognize that aberration is dependent entirely upon the velocity of an observer relative to the velocity of light, and that the velocity of a planet that is farther from the sun than the earth must be smaller than the velocity of the earth. Inner planets can be substituted for outer planets for variety, and the question can be made more difficult by requesting a quantitative answer.

Question (5) is an elegant illustration of SYNTHESIS, but it may be too difficult for students in the introductory course. Wien's radiation law for black-bodies is linked to the Doppler effect in this question. Some familiarity with differential calculus and how it is applied is needed to show that Wien's law leads to a fractional change of temperature that is equal to the fractional change of wavelength induced by the Doppler effect. The fractional change of wavelength is 10^{-4} and so the actual change of temperature observed is 3×10^{-4}K. The better students may not be able to see all the way to a final solution, but they should recognize that the effect of the motion must be to increase the apparent temperature in the direction of motion, and thus they have to decide only between choices (B) and (D). Instead of the orbital motion of the earth about the sun, one could specify the more important motion of the sun about the galaxy, approximating it as 300 km/sec for the purposes of the question. This brings the variation of the observed temperature to millikelvins which is actually observed.

Question (6) links the Coriolis effect and the weather, including cyclonic and anti-cyclonic flows. Furthermore, it requires a clear understanding of the hemispheric inversion on a rotating sphere.

In a "Walk Under the Night Sky" the interlocutor could raise the hypothetical issue of what the night sky might look like if the sun were located deep inside of a globular cluster. A considerable amount of SYNTHESIS is required to deal with this novelty. The absence of a "milky way", and of local interstellar dust, and the preponderance of densely packed red giants distributed over the entire sky would provide much food for thought.

EVALUATION

A detailed description of the meaning of EVALUATION in the context of General Education Science was given on Page 6 along with an example of one type of question designed to test for one facet of that skill. Often, but not always, EVALUATION requires that a comparison be made between two or more alternatives, and that a judgment be rendered. The concern of educators with the issue of EVALUATION is often focussed upon the ability to distinguish between science and pseudo-science, and with various religious beliefs that are inconsistent with scientific viewpoints. Equally important, however, for citizens who vote in a technological society, is an ability to evaluate two conflicting scientific arguments. Performance in this latter capacity generally hinges upon the ability to assess the reliability of data, the validity of assumptions, and the assertion of model-dependent facts. Testing strategies should therefore aim at those qualities.

1. All of the following statements are correct; but all except one is the result of a SELECTION EFFECT in the statistical sampling. Which one is NOT due to selection?

   A. Most stars on the original H-R diagram are more luminous than our sun.
   B. 35% of the brightest stars in the night sky are evolved red giants or supergiants.
   C. On a photograph of a cluster of galaxies, 70% are spirals.
   D. The average orbital period of all known eclipsing binaries is less than 10 days.
   E. Most of the nearest stars to the sun are less luminous than the sun.

2. Galileo's physics of motion described the path of a projectile as a parabola. What assumption produced that result?

   A. Projectiles do not accelerate while in flight.
   B. Neglect the effect of air resistance.
   C. Gravity is constant above the surface of Earth.
   D. Projectiles follow the curvature of the earth.
   E. No assumption is needed for that result.

3. A popular book claimed that a near alignment of planets would cause tidal disasters on the Earth. That claim was absurd because

   A. planets can never really be aligned.
   B. the moon blocks the effects of such planets.
   C. there is no gravity from other planets.
   D. tidal forces from planets are infinitesimal.
   E. the earth is solid and resists tidal stresses.

4. If the universe is 10 billion years old, and stars convert hydrogen into helium, why is there any hydrogen still remaining?

    A. The universe is only 6000 years old.
    B. There is almost no hydrogen still remaining.
    C. Helium is reconverted to hydrogen when stars die.
    D. Most hydrogen remains in interstellar gas clouds.
    E. Stars only convert 10% of their hydrogen into helium.

5. If stars have been EVOLVING by converting hydrogen into helium, why do they all have the same chemical composition?

    A. The universe is only 6000 years old.
    B. Conversion occurs only deep inside the cores.
    C. Interstellar hydrogen replenishes the supply.
    D. Stars do not appear to have the same composition.
    E. Convection keeps stars uniformly mixed.

6. If the universe is really expanding, why do galaxies not appear to get smaller every year?

    A. The universe is not expanding.
    B. Light does not travel in exactly straight lines.
    C. Galaxies are not all the same size.
    D. The variation is too small to measure.
    E. Sizes of galaxies expand at the same rate.

(See also the model-dependent/independent question on Pg.7.)

The intended answers are: 1-E; 2-C; 3-D; 4-E; 5-B; 6-D

Question (1) probes the subtleties of selection effects, and it can only be asked near the end of an astronomy course after the statistics of stars, binaries, and galaxies have been discussed. However, similar questions can be constructed within a more restricted topic area.

Question (2) is a good example of the need to be sensitive to the effects of a subtle assumption. It is distressing to see how many physics text books give a formal derivation of the path of a Galilean projectile as a parabola, without ever pointing out the assumption upon which it is based (and the fact that the assumption is false, and is in direct violation of the Newtonian theory of gravitation)! Many students who have taken an undergraduate physics course are convinced that the path of a (local) projectile is a parabola, and that it is a mathematically proven fact. Therefore, question (2) would be a challenge even for some physics students.

Question (3) makes reference to the pseudo-science book, "The Jupiter Effect", that preyed upon and exploited public ignorance; and questions (4), (5), and (6) are based directly upon some published arguments used by Biblical Fundamentalist Creationists to argue that the earth (and everything else) is no older than 6000 years. That assertion is given as the first choice for an answer in each case, to provide the format for EVALUATION since it is the correct choice for a Fundamentalist Christian. Most students will eliminate the naive Fundamentalist view, but the better part of critical thinking is to identify a good argument, and not merely to reject a poor one.

Since the model-dependent vs. model-independent format was given earlier, it was not repeated here. However, this is the most important aspect of the skill of EVALUATION. Although practicing scientists are keenly aware of the distinction, both in general and in their own work, they are often not cautious about blending the two in the heat of a discussion. Their colleagues instinctively sort out such blends, largely because they are aware of what things are models in their discipline. However, the lay public lacks such an awareness, and is easily deceived by what sounds like a cogent argument. Students in a one-semester general education science course cannot hope to gain such a sophisticated discriminatory sense, but with some practice it is possible to discern the general traits of model-dependent assertions. If nothing else, it is a mark of some distinction to be aware of the difference and to attempt to seek it out when EVALUATING a scientific presentation.

ARCHITECTURE OF QUESTIONS

In the previous section we considered the construction of questions designed to test for specific attributes under the general topic of the course. There are some principles of design that transcend the specific topics, and we now take up the general design of all questions regardless of the attributes that are being tested. The first of these general principles concerns the construction of the foils, i.e., those incorrect answers that are planted intentionally to conceal the correct answer.

THEORY OF THE FOILS

Creating the foils is probably the most challenging and time consuming aspect of the construction of multiple choice examination questions, and all the more so if they are to be done well. The basic design concept behind the foils is that they should serve a useful diagnostic function on an individual basis for students, and on a collective basis for the quality of the questions and of the examination as a whole.

There are some general principles that should first be enumerated prior to examining the diagnostic functions. The foils should conform as much as possible to the following design specifications.

1. A minimum of 5 choices should be used to keep the probability of success by random choice down to 20%. This provides a rough criterion for what constitutes a failing score. Since some questions involve only two choices, and have no foils, it is important that those with foils adhere to this statistic without compromise.

2. The foils should always be reasonable choices, or at least appear to be reasonable so as to prevent simple elimination by students who do not really comprehend the question.

3. The better students should be able to eliminate 3 of the 5 choices, but need to deliberate carefully with the remaining 2 choices.

4. The options, "none of the above", and "all of the above" should be used sparingly. Appropriate and inappropriate uses of these options will be discussed later.

5. All of the responses, including the correct one,

should be as short as it is possible to make them without compromising clarity or good grammar. If possible, they should be contained on a single line; words in common to all can be placed as part of the stated question.

6. Complete sentences and proper grammar should always be employed.

The diagnostic properties of the foils reside in their ability to aid the process of analyzing poor performance by a student on the examination as a whole. If the foils are created with some care, it should be possible to distinguish between students who have not been diligent in their studies, and those who have been diligent but who need additional instruction for clarification. In more restricted topic areas such as orbit mechanics, or light and radiation theory, etc., it should be possible to identify a specific type of misconception that persists with an individual student who is otherwise doing well.

Whenever a commonly held misconception is known, it should be incorporated directly as one of the foils. Classic examples are: the changing seasons on the earth is due to changes in the distance between the earth and the sun; artificial satellites remain in orbit because a centrifugal force balances the earth's gravitational force; astronauts are weightless because they have escaped from the gravitation of the earth. Other examples of common misconceptions are discussed in Physics Today, July 1984, Pg. 24 and September 1991, Pg. 56.

In cases where classic misconceptions are not prevalent, one of the foils should be a very reasonable, yet definitely incorrect option. The remaining foils should depart more from being reasonable alternatives, while never becoming totally absurd. A student who consistently selects unreasonable options without any discernible pattern divulges a failure to grasp the essence of the subject for reasons that can be explored by an interview. Conversely, one who displays a pattern of usually selecting the correct response, but often selecting the reasonable but incorrect response, needs some specific guidance, but little more. Much can be learned from the latter student in an interview in which he or she is asked to try to reconstruct the thinking that led to the choices of the incorrect foils. If the foils are constructed strategically, one might uncover a very specific misconception, such as failure to appreciate the fact that perfect black-bodies are perfect radiators as well as perfect absorbers. Another trait that can be discerned from the patterns of answers to properly designed questions is that of rote memorization of information with little or no comprehension.

When the option "none of the above" is used as a foil, it often means that the examiner was unable to construct enough substantive foils and has opted to use this device for no other purpose, either didactic or analytic. There is some merit to that if the device is to be used as a correct choice in some questions, for otherwise it will become apparent that whenever it appears it is the correct choice! When it is the correct choice, it has little didactic value unless its purpose is to call attention to several notably invalid ways to explain something. Otherwise, the student may be left with four incorrect explanations, which he certifies by selecting "none of the above", and is then left to wonder if there are any correct explanations. This device can be described as a "non-answer, answer" and as such it has no counterpart in essay type examinations. Students perceive it as intentional obfuscation, and well it may be in some cases, thereby making its use of questionable value for evaluation of knowledge or comprehension.

The converse device, "all of the above", used as an affirming mechanism is less objectionable, and may have some genuine didactic merit. This, too, should be used sparingly, and should be incorporated into some questions as a genuine foil to avoid a default condition. The device has the didactic merit of illustrating situations in which more than one factor is simultaneously present, or some similarity exists that might not have been apparent to students until asked in this particular manner. The following questions illustrate such uses of the device.

1. Why did astronomers fail to detect stellar parallax for centuries after Copernicus suggested to look for it as a test for heliocentrism?

   A. Stars are much more distant than was thought.
   B. Angle measuring devices were very crude.
   C. No good telescopes were available.
   D. Nobody knew which stars were actually nearest.
   E. All of the above were reasons for the failure.

2. Taken as an entire class, the outer planets (those beyond Mars) differ from the inner planets in

   A. mass.
   B. radius.
   C. rotation.
   D. chemical composition.
   E. all of the above.

3. A rainbow is a good example of

   A. the spectrum of black-body radiation.
   B. refraction.
   C. total internal reflection.
   D. decomposed white light.
   E. all of the above.

STATISTICS OF THE RESPONSES

Multiple choice examinations should always be machine-scored not only for the speed, accuracy, and convenience that is afforded, but also to obtain statistical data concerning the responses to each of the questions. Ambiguous questions, poor foils, or inadequate instruction can often be detected by a study of such statistics. This kind of analysis should be done every time that the questions are used, even if they have been in service for some time, but especially when new questions are introduced.

There is no single criterion for a good question, but generally such questions have more than 50% of the class giving the correct response, and the bulk of the others selecting a foil that was either the most reasonable alternative, or a prevalent misconception.

Some of the more common signs of a problematical question are the following.

1. A very large fraction of the class selecting the correct response (95% or more).

2. A very small fraction of the class selecting the correct response (less than 15%).

3. A large fraction of the class (50% or more) selecting a particular foil.

4. Uniformly distributed responses across most or all of the foils; i.e., nearly 20% of the class for each foil.

Situation (1) usually means a very easy question, or one whose foils are weak and easily eliminated. A few such questions are acceptable, but they should be examined to see if a change in wording of the question, or in one or more of the foils would be helpful to make the question useful for evaluation.

Situation (2) is ambiguous and requires further study. The question may be too difficult; or it may be poorly worded so as to be not understood or ambiguous; or the instruction on that topic may have been inadequate. A study of the statistics of the responses to the foils may clarify that somewhat.

Situation (3) usually means that the "correct" response was poorly written, so a reasonable foil appears better. This might also mean an inherent ambiguity in the way in which the question is posed. Generally, it is immediately apparent when the question is reviewed in light of the foil that is heavily selected. This is a common occurrence since the person who constructs the questions has a clear idea of what was intended, and rarely interprets things in the manner that students do.

Situation (4) usually points to inadequate instruction about the topic so that all of the foils appear reasonable.

Item analysis should be an ongoing process when multiple choice examinations are utilized, and improvements are always possible. Multiple versions of the same question should be kept in the testbank, and their statistics compared between different classes. A randomization scheme should be used to insure that no choice-letter is favored.

GRADES AND SCALE NORMALIZATION

The multiple choice examination produces an objective and unambiguous score for the performance of each student. The number of correct responses and the fraction of the total number that are correct is measured. However, the evaluation of that score as a measure of achievement toward the goals of the course is subjective. In most institutions that evaluation is expressed as a letter grade on a scale of five, often further subdivided into a scale of twelve. A methodology for making that evaluation less subjective is highly desirable.

One school of thought holds that an absolute scale can be established which then converts the absolute score into an absolute performance. Generally such a scale is defined as 90% and above being graded as an "A", 80% to 89% as a "B", 70% to 79% as a "C", 60% to 69% as a "D", and any score lower than 60% receives an "F" and is taken to be a failing performance. While those boundary values may be adjusted, the philosophy of this method assumes that all examinations are measuring-instruments that are calibrated to a common set of units. Scientists know that such calibration can be achieved only if the instruments can all be set to measuring one common quantity before they are used to measure a variety of different quantities. In the case of examinations given by different instructors, or even those given by the same instructor at different times, such an objective calibration is not feasible. Therefore, using this methodology is the equivalent of attempting to compare measurements of lengths that are done in centimeters by one person, with those done in inches by another. Nobody would consciously make such a comparison because it is customary to label such measurements with units, such as cm and in. However, grades are tacitly labeled as if they were on the same scale (percentage; or letter equivalent) and so the invalid comparison is often done unwittingly.

As an example, we might imagine gymnastics instructors testing children for their ability to jump. Each instructor places one of his own hands upon a wall as high as he can reach, and scores the performances as percentages of that height reached by the top of the head of each jumping child. Upon comparing notes, the shortest instructor finds that he always has far more "A" students than does the tallest instructor!

Since absolute calibration of examinations is generally not possible, the best solution to the problem of evaluation and intercomparison is relative scale normalization. This is accomplished by fitting a statistical probability distribution to the observed frequency distribution, in a process that is commonly known as grading on a curve. Most students do not know what this procedure means, nor how it is done, but they do seem to know that, like vitamin C, it is something that is good for them even if they have no concept of what it is!

Using this method, the measured score loses its typical meaning, and the performance of individual students is evaluated relative to the class as a whole. The assignment of performance grades is based upon a statistical model which, like any model, might not be a valid representation of the actual population. The standard model assumes that no unusual selection effects have operated to populate the class, and thus the performances of a large number of students will approach the random error distribution represented by the Gaussian distribution function.

The sample mean value then serves to normalize the scale of each examination, and the sample standard deviation measures the performance of the class on that examination. A grade of "C" is assigned to the mean score, and the other grades are assigned by an arbitrary criterion for how much departure from the mean score merits a different grade, either better or worse. This latter criterion is expressed in units of the standard deviation, and then it is called the Z-score. The assignment of a Z-score of +1 for a grade of "B", and +2 for a grade of "A" is as arbitrary and unjustified as assigning a percentage score of 80% for a grade of "B", and 90% for a grade of "A". A more rational, though still arbitrary, way of assigning the grades is to decide on the relative fraction of a class that should receive grades of "B" and "A" (and "D" and "F"). Such fractions then define the Z-scores at which the grades change, and the correct values can be found in a table that is usually called the "error function" (or erf) in most statistics textbooks. The table given below was constructed for a model in which 8% of the class is to receive a grade of "A", 16% "B", 53% "C", 15% "D", and 8% "F".

RANGE OF Z-SCORES	LETTER GRADE	FRACTION OF CLASS
Z > 1.4	A	8%
1.4 > Z > 0.7	B	16%
0.7 > Z > -0.8	C	53%
-0.8 > Z > -1.4	D	15%
-1.4 > Z	F	8%

The sample mean is computed from $M = 1/N \sum_{i}^{N} G_i$

The sample standard deviation is $S = \sqrt{(G_i - M)^2/(N - 1)}$

The symbology is: G_i = each score; M = mean of all scores; S = sample standard deviation; N = total number in sample.

The Z-score for each student is then given by the expression

$$Z_i = (G_i - M)/S$$

Actual scores can never be truly Gaussian for many reasons, but when N is large (more than 100) the approximation is reasonable. Formal statistical tests, such as the chi-square statistic, can be used to determine the goodness of fit, but a simple plot of binned scores is sufficient to assure that there is no significant departure from a random distribution. The histogram shown below was made from actual scores on one examination for a class in astronomy. The plotted theoretical Gaussian probability distribution was calculated by using the sample mean and the sample standard deviation. That procedure is only an approximation for visual display. The correct procedure involves the use of a non-linear least squares fitting algorithm. When proper fitting is done, the derived values for the (model) mean and standard deviation should be used

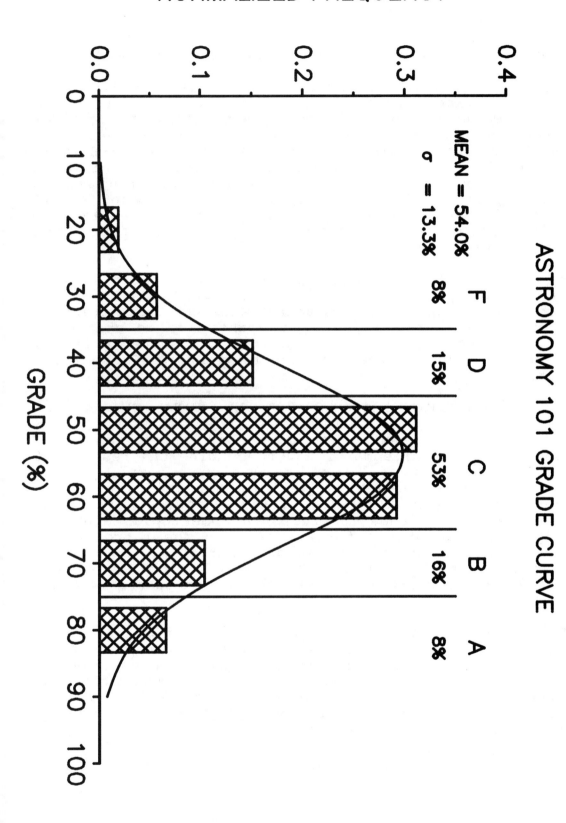

instead of the sample values to compute the Z-scores.

On the plotted graph, the percentages inscribed beneath each letter grade are the theoretical values that should result from the choice of Z-scores that define the vertical lines which are the cutoff values for each grade. The actual fractions in this particular class are: A 7%; B 10%; C 60%; D 15%; F 8%. One might decide, for example, that there are too many C grades, and not enough B grades resulting from the direct application of the formal criteria. A small adjustment of the Z-score criterion for the lower end of the B grades will correct that at once for this particular examination.

By using a method of this general sort, a table such as the one on the previous page can be published as part of the course description, so that students know how their relative performance will be graded. It might also be stated as policy that any small departures from the stated criteria will only be done if they affect the grades in a positive manner.

COMBINING EXAMINATION GRADES FOR A FINAL GRADE

The absolute percentage score method of assignment of grades leaves the dilemma of how to combine the results of all examinations since they are not on a common scale. Inevitably, one examination will be more difficult than another in the same sequence within a course, even when constructed by the same instructor. Some topics are more challenging than others for students in the introductory courses. Any direct arithmetic combination of examination scores is surely the equivalent of directly averaging distances that are given in centimeters with others that are given in inches.

The scale normalization that is achieved by fitting a Gaussian function to the distribution of scores eliminates this problem. In principle, it is possible to average the Z-scores that each student achieves on each examination for a final (mean Z-score) grade that can be assigned automatically from the table given previously. However, this is not the best way to proceed.

In moderate sized classes (more than 100, but fewer than 1000) the statistical fluctuations that occur naturally will disturb the tabular grade scale. Using the Z-score cutoff values given by the table, a particular examination may result in only 4% of the class obtaining a grade of "A", or some such anomaly. As indicated previously, this is readily corrected by making small adjustments in the actual Z-score cutoffs for each examination. Once that is done, however, the Z-scores are no longer normalized since they have slightly different meanings for each examination.

Therefore, the best procedure is to assign letter grades for each examination based upon the (modified) cutoffs for the Z-scores. The letter grades themselves correspond to numerical grade-points which define an absolutely normalized scale. The grade-point scale is (supposedly) universal among all American colleges and universities so as to permit transfers of students, and other intercomparisons. It is given by the following table:

A	4.0
A-	3.7
B+	3.3
B	3.0
B-	2.7
C+	2.3
C	2.0
C-	1.7
D+	1.3
D	1.0
D-	0.7
F	0.0

Thus, at the end of a term, a student will have a set of grade points corresponding to the various examinations, and the average of those values is a valid way to combine all of the performances for a final grade that is then taken from the table of grade-points given above. If examinations are to be weighted differently, those weights can now be applied directly to the grade-points as shown in the formula below

$$G = \sum_{i}^{N} (g_i w_i) / \sum_{i}^{N} w_i$$

where G is the final grade (point), and g_i are the

individual grade-points, and w_i are the weights. Spread sheets on modern personal computers are ideally suited to keeping these kinds of records and carrying out these calculations.

SIGNIFICANT FIGURES

Mathematical constants, such as pi, have an absolute value which, if it is not rational, requires an infinite number of digits following a decimal point to express. The decision to truncate such a constant and express it (approximately) as 3.141593 does not necessarily imply a lack of knowledge of successive digits beyond the 6th place of decimals, but rather a lack of concern for them in a given circumstance.

Measured physical quantities, however, are generally not known to unlimited accuracy, even when they refer to something that does have a unique and absolute value (such as the mass of a hydrogen atom). The statement of any such value with a limited number of decimal places is not a truncation for convenience, but rather an expression of the limit of knowledge. The expressed numbers are referred to as significant figures, and they define, implicitly, the limit of current knowledge of the absolute value of the quantity. Although this concept is elementary, it is violated in common usage. It is not uncommon, for example, to find a container of milk that states the contents as 1 pint, or equivalently, 0.473176 liters! Apparently, it is only the scientists who recognize the absurdity of this statement, and not those who produce or consume milk. The quantity is given originally to one significant figure, although more could be justified since the amount of milk is probably controlled to about 1%, and thus it should be stated as 1.00 pint. (It is equally common for those who are not familiar with the concept of significant figures to omit trailing zeros even when they are significant and convey important information.) However, the conversion of units to liters utilizes the defining conversion constant without regard to significance, and therefore inadvertently improves the implied accuracy of the contents of the container to parts per million!

Another common abuse of significant figures occurs when quantities with limited accuracy are combined by arithmetic operations, and herein lies the relevance to grades. If, for example, the sides of a cube are measured and found to have the lengths, 1.2 cm, 2.6 cm, and 4.4 cm, the volume of the cube found in student laboratory notebooks is likely to be 13.728 cm^3. The lengths of the sides are only known to 2 significant figures, but somehow they yield a volume that is implied as being known to 5 significant figures! Since arithmetic cannot increase the amount of information that is known, this is a violation of the use of significant figures to represent accuracy.

However, if a single quantity, such as a length, is measured repeatedly to a fixed accuracy, the mean value of all of the measured values is better determined than is any one of the measurements. Thus, the mean value of such an array can justifiably be specified to one more significant figure than are any of the measured values. The increased accuracy of the result does not come from the arithmetic, but rather from the <u>redundancy</u> of the measurements. It is this particular process that is generally misunderstood by all colleges and universities that specify grade-point averages (GPA) of students to three significant figures.

From the table, it is apparent that grade-points are quantities that are <u>defined</u> to have only two significant figures. A grade of B+, for example, has a grade-point equivalent of 3.3 and not 3.30. However, it is the practice of colleges and universities to average all of the grade-points from all of the courses that a student has taken, and then report the "grade-point average" (GPA) with 3 significant figures. This is an invalid procedure since it assumes that the same quantity is being measured by each course (i.e. the student him/herself). However, since most courses are independent and uncoupled (except for a sequence of mathematics, science, or other discipline specialty courses) the quantity that is measured by each course is the performance of the student in that particular specialty, and not his/her innate ability. In general, course grades measure different quantities, so if they are averaged the result can only be designated as a "characteristic" quantity and not a "better estimate" of performance. For example, if one were to measure the length of each and every table in a furniture store to the nearest centimeter, and then average all of those values, it would be absurd to state that result to the nearest millimeter (one additional significant figure) since no single table has been measured to that accuracy, and the mean value does not refer to any one table in the store (i.e., no redundancy). The average of the lengths of all of the tables in the store could be used only to "characterize" the lengths of tables that are sold in that store, and that quantity has little meaning without a specification of the variance of the lengths which measures their distribution around such a mean value.

A more poignant example of how this misconception of significant figures affects grades is had from a true case story at an unnamed college. A particular scholarship was awarded to those applicants who had a GPA of 3.8 or greater. One applicant had a GPA (reported by the Registrar) of 3.79. The scholarship committee consisted of a physicist, a mathematician, and a philosopher. The physicist argued that the scholarship should be awarded to this applicant since grade-points are measured quantities that have some uncertainty associated with them, and by an argument similar to the one I gave above, three significant figures cannot be justified for that quantity. The mathematician, however, argued that awarding the scholarship is equivalent to stating that 3.79 = 3.8, and that is certainly false. The philosopher argued that awarding the scholarship is the equivalent of altering a grade, and that is immoral. A good student lost a scholarship to numerical ignorance!

TEST BANK

Note: In writing up multiple choice exams, it is a good idea to put a statement at the beginning to the effect that "Students should choose the BEST answer of those given."

A few questions will require the instructor to draw or copy a small sketch of H-R diagrams, or astronomical objects.

Be sure to check that the indicated answers are correct! Typos can and do occur.

Introduction

1. Which is bigger. A) the Milky Way. or B) the Solar System?

2. The Local Group is
   A) our galaxy cluster.   B) another name for the planets between us and the Sun.
   C) the stars and gas in our spiral arm of the Milky Way.
   D) a group of asteroids near Jupiter.   E) none of the above.

3. The average distance between the Sun and Jupiter is 5.2 AU. Given that light travels 3×10^5 km in 1 second, the time it takes light to travel from the Sun to Jupiter is about
   A) 15.6 minutes.   B) 43.3 minutes.   C) 86.6 minutes.   D) 104 minutes.   E) 173 minutes.

4. The value of the astronomical unit (A.U.) is about
   A) 3×10^5 km.   B) 10^7 km.   C) 1.5×10^8 km.   D) 1.5×10^{10} km.   E) 10^{13} km.

5. The average distance between the Sun and Saturn is about 10 AU. Given that light travels 3×10^5 km in 1 second, the time it takes light to travel from the Sun to Saturn is about
   A) 33 minutes.   B) 83 minutes.   C) 142 minutes.   D) 250 minutes.   E) 375 minutes.

Chapter 1

1. Aristarchus is noted for having
   A) proposed that the Earth moves around the Sun.   B) measured the size of the Earth.
   C) measured the size of the Milky Way.   D) shown the Earth is round.
   E) explained what makes eclipses.

2. Seasons are caused by
   A) the Earth's distance from the Sun changing.
   B) the Sun's changing brightness during the sunspot cycle.
   C) the Earth's rotation axis being tipped so that first one hemisphere and then the other receives sunlight more directly.
   D) one side of the Sun being cooler than the other.
   E) none of the above.

3. On December 21 the Earth's rotation axis is tipped so that
   A) it is straight up and down (perpendicular) to the Earth's orbit.
   B) the north pole is tipped most nearly to the Sun.
   C) the north pole is tipped most strongly away from the Sun.
   D) the Sun shines exactly down on the south pole.
   E) the Sun shines exactly down on the equator.

4. If the Moon were new today and you could see it, at about what time would it rise?
    (A picture will help you figure this out.)
    A) midnight   B) dawn   C) sunset   D) noon   E) 3AM

5. Kepler is noted for
    A) being first to use a telescope to study the heavens.
    B) reviving and strongly advocating the heliocentric theory.
    C) discovering the moons of Jupiter.   D) formulating his laws of planetary motion.
    E) all of the above except D).

6. If you wanted to find Uranus in the night sky, you'd look for it near
    A) the zodiac. B) the celestial pole. C) the celestial equator. D) the zenith. E) the horizon.

7. Copernicus is noted for
    A) being first to use a telescope to study the heavens.
    B) reviving and strongly advocating the heliocentric theory.
    C) discovering the moons of Jupiter.
    D) formulating laws of planetary motion and gravity
    E) all of the above except D)

8. Newton is noted for
    A) being first to use the telescope. B) inventing calculus. C) discovering the law of gravity.
    D) being first to suggest that Earth moves around the Sun.   E) only B) and C).

9. From a Lunar eclipse the ancient Greeks deduced
    A) the shape of the Earth. B) the size of the Moon compared to the Earth.
    C) the temperature of the Sun.
    D) that the Earth was at the center of the Universe.   E) Only A) and B).

10. One AU is
    A) the distance from the Earth to the Moon. B) 1 million kilometers. C) 10 light years.
    D) the distance from the Earth to the Sun. E) the diameter of the Milky Way.

11. The Moon is a very thin crescent on the night of November 13th.
    On what day (approximately) will it be full?
    A) December 13.   B) November 27.   C) November 20. D) December 5. E) December 27.

12. One reason the ancient Greeks rejected the idea that the Earth moved around the Sun was that they
    A) could see no shift in star positions (parallax) over the course of the year.
    B) thought the Earth was flat and unable to move.
    C) thought the Earth was much bigger than the Sun.
    D) thought that the Earth was so light compared to the material of which heavenly bodies were made
        that it would fall apart if it moved.
    E) All of the above but A).

13. A planet moves a round the Sun in a circular orbit with a period of 27 years. How far is it from the Sun?
    A) 27 AU. B) 1/27 AU. C) 5.25 AU D) 3 AU. E) 9 AU.

14. Eratosthenes measured the size of the Earth by
    A) sailing a ship around it.
    B) measuring the size of its shadow at a Solar eclipse.
    C) measuring the length of shadows at different locations on Earth a known distance apart.
    D) measuring how long it took the Moon to complete an orbit around the Earth.
    E) measuring the Earth's force of gravity on the Moon.

Match the astronomer with discovery/contribution.
15. Copernicus   A) Developed theory of epicycles.
16. Kepler   B) Discovered planets move in ellipses, not circles.
17. Newton   C) Discovered phases of Venus and Jupiter's moons.
18. Ptolemy   D) First of this group to propose Earth and planets move around Sun.
19. Galileo   E) Developed mathematical laws of motion and theory of gravity.

20. The ecliptic is
    A) the Sun's path across the celestial sphere.
    B) the path across the celestial sphere followed by comets.
    C) the line on the celestial sphere directly above the Earth's equator.
    D) the point directly overhead.
    E) the line that divides the sky into the northern and souther half.

21. The summer solstice occurs on or about
    A) March 21.   B) June 21.   C) September 21.   D) December 21.   E) July 15th.

22. At the summer solstice
    A) day and night are of equal length.   B) autumn begins.   C) the Sun crosses the celestial equator.
    D) the Sun is the farthest north it gets in the sky.   E) The sun rises due east and sets due west.

23. Which of the following astronomers first proposed that the Earth orbited the Sun?
    A) Ptolemy.   B) Eratosthenes.   C) Kepler.   D) Copernicus.   E) Newton.

24. What is an epicycle supposed to explain?
    A) Solar eclipses.   B) Seasons.   C) Phases of the Moon.
    D) Retrograde motion of the planets.   E) Precession.

25. You wake during the night and see the Moon's left half lit and that the Moon is halfway across the sky from east to west. The time must be about
    A) Midnight.   B) 9 PM.   C) 3AM.   D) 6AM - just before it starts getting light.   E) 6PM.

26. The observed position of the Sun relative to the background stars changes each day because of
    A) the rotation of the Earth.
    B) the revolution of the Earth around the Sun.
    C) the actual motion of the Sun through space.
    D) the tilt of the Earth's axis.
    E) none of the above.

27. At the vernal equinox
    A) day-time and night-time are each approximately 12 hours long at all locations on Earth.
    B) the Sun rises directly in the east and sets directly in the west.
    C) it is the beginning of spring in the northern hemisphere.
    D) All of the above.
    E) Both A and C.

28. Which of the following statements about retrograde motion of a planet is incorrect?
   A) Retrograde motion is observed for both superior and inferior planets.
   B) A superior planet exhibits retrograde motion when it is near opposition.
   C) When the geocentric view was prevalent, the concept of epicycle motion was introduced to explain the retrograde motion.
   D) In the heliocentric system, retrograde motion arises because the planet that is closer to the Sun completes one orbit around the Sun in a shorter time.
   E) None of the above.

29. We know that the Earth revolves around the Sun because
   A) there is daytime and nighttime on Earth.
   B) the Sun rises in the east and sets in the west.
   C) the Earth's axis is tilted by 23.5.
   D) the position of sunrise relative to the background stars moves by about 1° each day.
   E) in the winter it is cold in the northern hemisphere and warm in the southern hemisphere.

30. The full moon
   A) rises at around sunset.
   B) is seen when the Moon and the Sun are on opposite sides of the Earth.
   C) always occurs at the middle of each month.
   D) All of the above.
   E) Both A and B.

31. Which of the following statements about retrograde motion of a planet is incorrect?
   A) A superior planet exhibits retrograde motion when it is near opposition.
   B) An inferior planet exhibits retrograde motion when it is near inferior conjunction.
   C) When the geocentric view was prevalent, the concept of epicycle motion was introduced to explain the retrograde motion.
   D) None of the above.

32. When Jupiter is at opposition, its angular diameter is measured by us to be 0.8 minutes of arc. Given that 1 radian has 57.3 degrees, and 1 degree has 60 minutes of arc, the angular diameter of Jupiter in radians is
   A) 0.00008   B) 0.00012   C) 0.00023   D) 0.00045   E) 0.007

33. At that time the distance between Jupiter and Earth is 4.1 AU or 6.15×10^8 km. Given that linear diameter = angular diameter x distance, the linear diameter of Jupiter is about
   A) 280,000 km.   B) 140,000 km.   C) 74,000 km.   D) 50,000 km.   E) 30,000 km.

34. The person who made accurate and continuous observations of the positions of stars and planets over a long period of time was
   A) Nicolaus Copernicus.   B) Tycho Brahe.   C) Johannes Kepler.
   D) Galileo Galilei.   E) Isaac Newton.

35. Among the contributions of Copernicus to astronomy are
   A) determination of the sidereal periods of the planets.
   B) working out a scale model of the solar system.
   C) discovery of the relation between the orbital period of a planet and its orbit size.
   D) all of the above.
   E) both A and B.

36. In orbiting around the Sun, a planet
    A) is moving faster when it is closer to the Sun.
    B) is moving slower when it is closer to the Sun.
    C) is constantly accelerating.
    D) Both A and C are correct.
    E) Both B and C are correct.

37. An asteroid is located between Mars and Jupiter. The semi-major axis of the asteroid's orbit around the Sun is 4 AU. From Kepler's third law, the sidereal period of the asteroid's orbit is _____ years.

    A) 2   B) 4   C) 8   D) 16   E) 64

38. Which of the following is not a contribution made by Galilei to science?
    A) The demonstration that heavy and light objects fall at the same rate to the ground.
    B) The finding that a planet's distance from the Sun is related to its orbital period.
    C) The discovery of 4 moons of Jupiter.
    D) The discovery of the phases of Venus.
    E) The discovery that the Milky Way consists of numerous faint stars.

39. An asteroid is located between Mars and Jupiter. The semi-major axis of the asteroid's orbit around the Sun is 3 AU. From Kepler's Third law, $P^2 = a^3$, the sidereal period of the asteroid's orbit is about _____ years.
    A) 3.3   B) 5.2   C) 10.5   D) 15.8   E) 27.0

40. For hundreds of years after Copernicus suggested searching for stellar parallax, astronomers failed to discover it. Why?
    A) Stars are very much farther away than was thought.
    B) Angle measuring devices were too crude.
    C) No telescopic devices were available.
    D) Nobody knew which stars were the closest ones.
    E) All of the above were the reasons.

41. In his measurement of the circumference of the Earth, Eratosthenes made all but one of the following assumptions. The assumption he didn't need was
    A) The shape of the Earth is a sphere.
    B) The Earth spins (rotates) on an axis.
    C) The Sun is very distant from the Earth.
    D) The distance between Syene and Alexandria is known.
    E) Light always travels along straight lines.

42. One of the most difficult problems for ancient astronomers to explain was the
    A) cause of the seasons.
    B) annual motion of the Sun on the ecliptic.
    C) phases of the Moon.
    D) eclipses of the Sun.
    E) retrograde motions of the planets.

43. Ancient astronomers were aware of only the stars they could see with their unaided eyes. Approximately how many such stars are visible in the entire sky?
    A) 10,000   B) millions.   C) billions.   D) hundreds of billions.   E) just a few hundred.

44. The Copernicus's model of the heavens destroyed many of the concepts of the heavens held by the ancient Greeks. One that his work retained was
    A) The Earth is at the center of the Universe.
    B) The Sun controls all motions of the planets.
    C) All celestial motions occur at uniform speeds.
    D) All celestial orbits are circles.
    E) Gravitation.

45. Which of the following observations constitutes a critical test for the motion of the Earth around the Sun?
    A) The shape of the shadow of the Earth in lunar eclipses.
    B) Phase changes of the planet Venus.
    C) Phase changes of the Moon going around the Earth.
    D) Unequal durations of our four seasons.
    E) Parallax of stars.

46. The retrograde motion of a planet in the sky arises because
    A) planets move faster if they are farther from the Sun.
    B) planets move slower if they are farther from the Sun.
    C) all planets move at the same speed.
    D) the orbits of the planets are not circles.
    E) planets reverse their motion when near the Earth.

47. Determining the distances to celestial objects generally involves the evaluation of
    A) gigantic triangles.
    B) synodic periods.
    C) brightness of objects.
    D) sizes of objects.
    E) colors of objects.

48. Kepler was convinced that the sizes of the orbits of the planets were derived by God from
    A) the prime numbers.
    B) the square roots of integers.
    C) the cubes of integers.
    D) the regular polygons.
    E) the regular polyhedrons.

49. Based on Kepler's third law you can be sure that the orbital period of a very distant planet like Pluto must be
    A) very much longer than the orbit period of the Earth.
    B) very much shorter than the orbit period of the Earth.
    C) nearly equal to the orbit period of the Earth.
    D) impossible to estimate without direct measurement.
    E) related to the eccentricity of its orbit.

50. Kepler found that a planet moves in its orbit with a speed that
    A) is proportional to its distance from the Sun.
    B) is inversely proportional to its distance from the Sun.
    C) is inversely proportional to its distance from the center of the orbit.
    D) is constant when viewed from the unoccupied focus.
    E) sweeps out equal areas in equal intervals of time.

51. Which of the following did Galileo discover with his telescope?
    A) Craters on the Moon.
    B) Phases of the planet Venus.
    C) Spots on the Sun.
    D) Moons around the planet Jupiter.
    E) All of the above.

52. Which of Galileo's observations strongly suggested that the Sun is at the center of the Solar System?
    A) Craters on the Moon.
    B) Phases of the planet Venus.
    C) Spots on the Sun.
    D) Moons around the planet Jupiter.
    E) All of the above.

53. Which of the following is NOT caused by the rotation of the Earth?
    A) Wind circulation around storms and high and low pressure regions.
    B) The rising and setting of the Moon.
    C) The rising and setting of the Sun.
    D) The motion of the Sun along the ecliptic.
    E) The operation of a Sundial.

54. A critical test demonstrating that the Earth is a sphere is observing
    A) that there is a horizon.
    B) that the entire sky moves around us.
    C) the Earth's shadow on any one eclipse of the Moon.
    D) the Earth's shadow at all eclipses of the Moon.
    E) many eclipses of the Sun.

55. A critical test demonstrating that the Earth revolves around the Sun is the observation of
    A) the changing of the seasons.
    B) the parallax of the stars.
    C) the variation of the apparent size of the Sun.
    D) the Coriolis effect.
    E) the motion of the Sun along the ecliptic.

ESSAY 1

1. You can tell that Jupiter is at opposition by noting that
   A) it rises at midnight.
   B) it crosses the north-south line passing straight overhead at midnight.
   C) it sets at midnight.
   D) it is to the east of the constellation Orion.
   E) it is to the west of the constellation Orion.

2. The latitude of Washington, D.C. is 38 degrees. If the President were to look at Polaris one night, she would find that its altitude is
   A) 38 degrees.   B) 45 degrees.   C) 52 degrees.   D) 66.5 degrees.   E) 23.5 degrees.

3. Which planet below can never be seen at midnight?
   A) Venus   B) Mars   C) Jupiter   D) Saturn   E) Both A and B.

Chapter 2

1. Newton's law of gravity is
   A) $F = GMm/r^2$.   B) $F = GMMr^2$.   C) $F = GMm/r$.
   D) $F = GMr^2/m$.   E) none of the above.

2. What force holds the planets in their orbits around the Sun?
   A) Electric   B) Magnetic   C) Rotational   D) Gravitational   E) Nuclear

3. The law of inertia states that
   A) Planets move in circles round the Sun.   B) Planets move in ellipses around the Sun.
   C) Objects generally move in ellipses unless forces act on them.
   D) Objects remain at rest or move in straight lines at constant velocity unless a net force acts on them.
   E) None of the above.

4. Your seat belt prevents you crashing forward into the dashboard when the car suddenly stops. Your forward motion before your belt saved you is an example of
   A) Newton's law of inertia.
   B) Newton's law of $F = MA$.
   C) Newton's law that every action has an equal and opposite reaction.
   D) Newton's law of universal gravitation.
   E) None of the above.

5. The ability of a rocket to move through the vacuum of space by firing its engine demonstrates
   A) that orbits are ellipses.
   B) Newton's law of inertia.
   C) Kepler's Third law.
   D) Newton's law that every action has an equal and opposite reaction.
   E) Newton's law of universal gravitation.

6. Suppose you are an astronaut taking a space walk to fix your spacecraft with a hammer. Your life-line breaks and the jets on your backpack are out of fuel. How would you return to your craft safely (without the help of someone else)?
    A) Kick your feet in a cyclic pattern.
    B) Fling your arms around in circles.
    C) Throw the hammer in disgust at the spaceship.
    D) Throw the hammer away from the spaceship.
    E) Kiss your ship goodbye.

7. The mass of Venus is 0.8 times the mass of the Earth. The mean distance of Venus from the Sun is 0.7 AU. The gravitational force between the Sun and Venus is _____ times the gravitational force between the Sun and the Earth.
    A) 0.88   B) 1.14   C) 1.63   D) 2.33   E) 2.92

8. The mass of Jupiter is 318 times the mass of the Earth. Jupiter's mean distance from the Sun is 5.2 AU. The gravitational force between the Sun and Jupiter is about _____ times the gravitational force between the Sun and the Earth.
    A) 2   B) 12   C) 60   D) 300   E) 0.5

9. According to Newton's second law of motion, an unbalanced force changes an object's
    A) position. B) speed. C) mass. D) momentum.   E) All of the above except C).

10. According to Newton's laws, an object moving on a circle
    A) requires a force to deflect its motion into a curved path.
    B) experiences an acceleration.
    C) will fly radially outward away from the center of the circle if the force holding it ceases.
    D) will fall radially inward toward the center of the circle if the force holding it ceases.
    E) Only A) and B).

11. Newton's law of gravitation is proportional to the product of the two masses that create the force and
    A) is universally constant.
    B) increases with the square of increasing separation.
    C) decreases with the square of increasing separation.
    D) decreases with the square of increasing time.
    E) depends on the chemical composition of the masses.

12. The Sun is 300,000 times as massive as the Earth. According to Newton's physics the force of the Sun upon the Earth is
    A) 300,000 times greater than that of the Earth upon the Sun.
    B) 150,000 times greater than that of the Earth upon the Sun.
    C) equal to that of the Earth upon the Sun.
    D) balanced by the centrifugal force of the Earth's motion.
    E) the Earth does not exert a force upon the Sun.

13. According to Newton's laws of motion, the Moon remains in orbit around the Earth because
    A) the gravity of the Earth pulls it toward the Earth.
    B) its velocity cancels the gravity of the Earth.
    C) the Sun's gravity balances the Earth's gravity.
    D) the original motion of the Moon was circular.
    E) the Earth's magnetic field holds it there.

14. Which of Kepler's laws are followed by a space vehicle in orbit around the Sun?
    A) Kepler's first law.   B) Kepler's second law.   C) Kepler's third law.
    D) All three of Kepler's laws.   E) None of Kepler's laws.

15. If instead of the Earth the Sun had a binary companion star in our same orbit having the same mass as the Sun itself, the orbital period of such a binary would be
    A) 2 years.   B) 0.5 years.   C) 0.7 years.   D) 1.4 years.
    E) the same as the current period of the Earth (365 days).

16. An artificial satellite in a circular orbit just above the Earth's surface moves at about 18,000 mi/hr. Saturn has about 100 times the mass of the Earth, and about 9 times the radius of the Earth. At what speed must a satellite move to stay in circular orbit just above the surface of Saturn?
    A) 42,000 mi/hr.   B) 60,000 mi/hr.   C) 36,000 mi/hr.   D) 18,000 mi/hr.   E) 86,000 mi/hr.

17. If a space probe were launched such that it would fall into the Sun along a straight path, about how long would it take to get to the Sun?
    A) 365 days.   B) 182 days.   C) 96 days.   D) 64 days.   E) 42 days.

18. The Earth is nearest to the Sun during our winter season in the northern hemisphere. From this fact and by applying Kepler's second law we can deduce that the shortest season in the northern hemisphere is
    A) winter.   B) spring.   C) summer.   D) fall.
    E) each season is exactly one quarter of a year.

19. The planet Saturn has billions of tiny particles orbiting it, forming a disk of rings. According to Kepler's third law
    A) the innermost ring must have the shortest period.
    B) the outermost ring must have the shortest period.
    C) all the rings must have the same period.
    D) Kepler's laws apply only to planets orbiting the Sun.
    E) the rings should move like a rigid disk.

20. A popular book recently claimed that a near alignment of the planets would cause tidal disasters on Earth. That claim was known to be absurd because
    A) planets can never actually be aligned.
    B) the Moon blocks the effects of such alignments.
    C) there is no gravitational effect on us from other planets.
    D) Earth is solid and impervious to tidal effects.
    E) the gravitational and tidal forces from other planets on us are so extremely tiny.

21. Pushing a shopping cart is much easier to do than pushing an automobile. Write the letter corresponding to the equations below that expresses this fact.
    A) $P^2 = a^3$.   B) $F = ma$.   C) $F = GMm/r^2$.   D) $D = vt$.   E) $A = \pi r^2$.

22. Halley's comet orbits the Sun with a period of 75 years. Write the letter of the equation below that would be used to calculate the size (semi-major axis) of the orbit of that comet.
    A) $P^2 = a^3$.   B) $F = ma$.   C) $F = GMm/r^2$.   D) $D = vt$.   E) $A = \pi r^2$.

Chapter 3
1. Which has the higher energy   A) red light or   B) blue light?

2. Which has the longer wavelength   A) an x-ray or   B) visible light?

3. One atom contains two protons and two orbiting electrons while another
   has one proton and one orbiting electron. The atoms are
   A) helium and oxygen   B) hydrogen and helium   C) helium and nitrogen
   D) helium and carbon   E) hydrogen and carbon

4. The spectrum of a typical star like our Sun shows
   A) mostly bright emission lines.   B) No spectral lines at all.   C) mostly dark absorption lines.

5. Particles of light are sometimes called
   A) protons.   B) neutrons.   C) electrons.   D) Partons.   E) photons.

6. Which wavelength of light carries more energy   A) a radio wave or   B) an ultraviolet wave.

7. If you move toward a light source rapidly its light will look
   A) bluer.   B) redder.   C) dimmer.   D) cooler.   E) None of the above.

8. How long does it take light to travel from Earth to Mars? Assume Mars is 0.5 AU from Earth and that 1 AU is 1.5×10^8 km. The speed of light is 3×10^5 km/sec.
   A) 25 minutes.   B) 250 seconds.   C) 25 seconds.   D) 0.003 seconds.   E) 30 seconds.

9. Radio waves differ from visible light in that they
   A) travel much faster through empty space.   B) travel much slower through empty space.
   C) have a much longer wavelength.   D) have a much shorter wavelength.
   E) are not electromagnetic waves like light is.

10. Wien's law relates
    A) an object's speed to its mass.
    B) the color of radiation to the temperature of the body emitting it.
    C) the shape of an orbit to its distance from the Sun.
    D) the wavelength of light to its distance.
    E) the wavelength of light to its velocity.

11. Astronomers can measure what stars are made of by
    A) seeing what spectrum lines they show.   B) weighing the light they emit.
    C) measuring the speed of the light they emit.   D) weighing them using Kepler's law.
    E) measuring how fast they are moving.

12. The spectrum of the Orion nebula shows only bright emission lines. From that we can conclude that it is
    A) a reflection nebula.   B) a cloud of hot gas.   C) composed of millions of individual stars.
    D) either A) or C)   E) none of the above

13. Which of the following correctly orders the radiation of the electromagnetic spectrum by wavelength (from large to small) ?
    A) x-ray, radio, ultraviolet, visible, infrared, gamma ray.
    B) infrared, x-ray, visible, radio, gamma ray, ultraviolet.
    C) visible, infrared, gamma ray, ultraviolet, radio, x-ray.
    D) radio, infrared, visible, ultraviolet, x-ray, gamma ray.
    E) gamma ray, ultraviolet, x-ray, radio, visible, infrared.

14. Which has the shorter wavelength   A) ultraviolet or   B) infrared radiation?

15. Visible light has a wavelength of about
    A) 10 nm   B) 100 nm   C) 50 nm.   D) 500 nm.   E) 5000 nm.

16. The throwing of a ball (with a beeper inside) across the classroom is an attempt to demonstrate
    A) Newton's first law of motion.
    B) the Doppler effect.
    C) the particle nature of light.
    D) the relation between force and acceleration.
    E) None of the above.

17. A galaxy is moving directly away from us at a speed of 0.2c. If the galaxy emits radiation at a wavelength of 300 nm, we will observe the radiation at a wavelength of _____ nm.
    A) 600   B) 360   C) 300   D) 240   E) 200

18. Electromagnetic radiation
    A) refers to just the light we see.
    B) propagates in vacuum at a speed of 3×10^{12} km per sec.
    C) affects electrons but not protons.
    D) is generated when a charged particle accelerates.
    E) is also known as cosmic rays.

19. Electromagnetic radiation is distinguished by
    A) its wavelength.
    B) its frequency.
    C) its color.
    D) A and B are both correct.
    E) A, B, and C are all correct.

20. The demonstration of the laser beam and chalk dust illustrates
    A) the scattering of light.
    B) the different colors of light.
    C) the wave nature of light.
    D) the Doppler effect.
    E) none of the above.

21. In order of increasing frequency, the classifications of electromagnetic radiation are ordered as
    A) Gamma-ray, X-ray, ultraviolet, optical, infrared, radio.
    B) radio, infrared, ultraviolet, optical, X-ray, gamma-ray.
    C) infrared, optical, radio, X-ray, ultraviolet, gamma-ray.
    D) radio, optical, infrared, ultraviolet, X-ray, gamma-ray.
    E) radio, infrared, optical, ultraviolet, X-ray, gamma-ray.

22. Which of the following statements about the radiation emitted by matter is NOT correct?
    A) A hot solid produces a continuum spectrum.
    B) A hot, diffuse gas produces an emission line spectrum.
    C) Each element has its own characteristic line spectrum.
    D) All of the above.
    E) `None of the above.

23. The wavelength of red light is about 700 nm. The frequency of red light is about _____ Hz.
    A) 4×10^{11} B) 7×10^{12} C) 2×10^{13} D) 4×10^{14} E) 2×10^{16}

24. In the hydrogen atom, the electron and proton are bound together by
    A) gravitational force.   B) nuclear force.   C) electromagnetic force.
    D) chemical force.   E) none of the above.

25. The red line that you see in the demonstration of the hydrogen spectrum corresponds to the transition of the electron in the hydrogen atom from
    A) level n=2 to level n=1.   B) level n=3 to level n=1.   C) level n=3 to level n=2.
    D) level n=4 to level n=2.   E) level n=1 to level n=2.

26. The frequency of an optical photon is about 5×10^{14} Hz. The frequency of an infrared photon is about 10^{13} Hz. The energy of the optical photon is _____ times the energy of the infrared photon.
    A) 20   B) 50   C) 200   D) 400   E) 5000

27. The orbital velocity of the Earth is 30 km/s and the velocity of light is 300,000 km/s. By approximately how much can our orbital speed change the wavelength of H-alpha (656.3 nm) coming from a nearby star?
    A) 15 nm.   B) 35 nm.   C) 0.03 nm.   D) 0.0656 nm.   E) 1 nm.

28. Microwave radiation is very useful for cooking because
    A) microwaves are reflected by metals.
    B) microwaves are absorbed by water.
    C) microwaves travel at the speed of light.
    D) microwaves are stationary waves.
    E) microwaves cannot be seen.

29. When you switch off the lights in your room at night, the walls, ceiling, and floor are at a temperature of about 300 K. Why are you not dazzled by the radiation that they emit?
    A) Because they do not emit any radiation.
    B) Because they are not anything like black-bodies.
    C) Nothing can radiate below a temperature of 3000 K.
    D) Human eyes cannot see infrared radiation.
    E) Human eyes cannot see ultraviolet radiation.

Use the following code to describe the kind of radiation coming from each of the following sources.
    A) BLACK-BODY RADIATION   B) EMISSION LINE (or NOT Black-body)
30. automobile headlights.
31 neon advertising signs.
32. sodium vapor street lamps.
33. sunlight.
34. fluorescent light tubes.
35. glowing lava from a volcano.

36. Which of the equations listed below describes the total amount of energy emerging from each unit of area on the surface of a hot black-body?
    A) $E = \sigma T^4$ B) $\Delta\lambda/\lambda = v/c$ C) $\lambda = 3 \times 10^6/T$ D) $B = L/(4\pi r^2)$ E) $L = 4\pi r^2 \sigma T^4$

37. Which of the equations listed below provides most of our knowledge of the sizes of the stars?
    A) $E = \sigma T^4$ B) $\Delta\lambda/\lambda = v/c$ C) $\lambda = 3 \times 10^6/T$ D) $B = L/(4\pi r^2)$ E) $L = 4\pi R^2 \sigma T^4$

38. A perfect black-body is NOT capable of
    A) reflecting light.   B) absorbing infrared radiation.   C) emitting visible light.
    D) emitting radio waves.   E) emitting all the colors of a rainbow.

39. The Sun is like a black-body radiating at a temperature of about 6000 K. The brightest wavelength emitted by the Sun is about 500 nm. What would be the brightest wavelength emitted by a star whose temperature is 30,000 K ?
    A) 10 nm   B) 30 nm   C) 50 nm   D) 100 nm   E) 300 nm

40. A perfect black body at a temperature of 6000 K emits more radiation than a perfect black body at 5000 K
    A) only at ultraviolet wavelengths.
    B) only at infrared wavelengths.
    C) only at visible wavelengths.
    D) at all wavelengths.
    E) no radiation is emitted by perfect black bodies.

ESSAY 2 LIGHT IN THE ATMOSPHERE

1. Refraction of light is a demonstration that the velocity of light inside glass must be
    A) the same as it is in free space.
    B) faster than it is in free space.
    C) slower than it is in free space.
    D) variable along its path.
    E) unmeasurable.

Chapter 4

1. How do we know what the core of the Earth is made of?
    A) Its high density gives us clues.
    B) Earthquake waves give information about the kind of material.
    C) Deep bore holes allow us to sample all but the inner 10% of the Earth.
    D) Solar neutrinos penetrate the Earth and allow us to take "x-ray" like pictures.
    E) Both A) and B) give evidence.

2. According to one hypothesis, from where did the Earth's atmosphere come?
    A) It was captured from the solar wind.
    B) It was gas swept up from the solar nebula as the Earth formed.
    C) Sunlight broke down surface rock liberating oxygen and water.
    D) Volcanic eruptions created the basic mix which has then been modified by sunlight, rain, and plant life.
    E) It was captured from Venus long ago when the Earth approached Venus too closely.

3. We believe that the Earth's core is _____ because of _____.
    A) solid silicates   deep bore holes drilled in Russia.
    B) solid iron   deep bore holes drilled in the USA.
    C) molten silicate   earthquake wave studies.
    D) molten iron   earthquake wave studies.
    E) hydrogen   gas vented from the core.

4. Aurora are created by
    A) meteor showers.
    B) gases in the upper atmosphere heated by collisions with solar particles.
    C) sunlight reflected off dust in the high atmosphere.
    D) emission of light by the ozone layer.   E) none of the above.

5. The present widening of the Atlantic Ocean is caused by
    A) gravitational forces exerted on the Earth by the Moon.
    B) the Earth expanding as its core material expands as a result of it gradually losing heat.
    C) the tidal force on the Earth exerted by the Sun.
    D) plate tectonic motions associated with convection in the Earth's interior.
    E) magnetic pressure that builds up in the earth as it spins.

6. The core of the Earth formed by
    A) asteroids hitting the earth and penetrating its crust to the core.
    B) the Earth's magnetic field pulling iron to the center.
    C) the denser iron sinking to the center as the Earth melted.
    D) the Moon's gravity pulling the lighter rocky material to the surface.
    E) the rocky material sinking to the center while the denser material was carried to the surface by convection.

7. The Earth is about how many years old?
    A) 5 million   B) 10 million   C) 100 million   D) 500 million   E) 5 billion

8. The carbon dioxide and water in the Earth's atmosphere came from
    A) the Sun's outer atmosphere.   B) nuclear reactions in the earth's core.
    C) volcanic eruptions.   D) sunlight breaking up hydrogen and turning it into other elements.
    E) None of the above.

9. Suppose the Earth's rotation axis was not tilted. How would this affect the number of hours of daylight?
   A) There would be more daylight in summer and less in winter.
   B) There would be fewer hours of daylight in summer than in winter.
   C) It would not alter the present situation.
   D) The number of hours of daylight would be the same throughout the year.
   E) It would not affect the number of hours of daylight, but it would make the day only 12 hours long.

10. The seasons of the Earth result from
    A) the varying speed of the Earth in its orbit.
    B) the Earth being farther from the Sun in winter because of its elliptical orbit.
    C) the tilt of the Earth's axis.
    D) the precession of the Earth's axis.
    E) none of the above.

11. In a few thousand years, the Earth's axis of rotation will not be pointing towards the star Polaris. This is because
    A) the rotation of the Earth is slowing down.
    B) the strength of the tides is increasing.
    C) the Earth's axis is precessing.
    D) the solar system will be on the other side of the Galaxy.
    E) All of the above.

12. The Earth's diameter is 27 miles larger at the equator than at the poles. This is because
    A) the Sun's gravitational force is larger at the Earth's equator than at the poles.
    B) the ocean tides are higher at the equator.
    C) the Earth is rotating.
    D) the rocks are softer at the poles.
    E) None of the above.

13. Which of the following statements about the precession of the Earth's axis is incorrect?
    A) It is caused by the gravitational pull of both the Sun and Moon on the equatorial bulge of the Earth.
    B) During the precession the angle of the tilt of the Earth's axis (23.5 degrees) does not change.
    C) The period of the precession is 26,000 years.
    D) It causes a precession of the position of vernal equinox on the Earth's orbit.
    E) None of the above.

14. As the Earth's axis precesses
    A) the angle of the tilt of the Earth's axis changes from 23.5 degrees to 0 degrees.
    B) the angle of the tilt of the Earth's axis changes from 23.5 degrees to 90 degrees.
    C) the angle of the tilt does not change; only the direction changes.
    D) both the angle and direction of the tilt change.
    E) neither the angle nor direction of the tilt changes.

15. Which of the following statements about the Earth is incorrect?
    A) It has an iron core.
    B) Its crust is divided into huge plates that jostle each other in a phenomenon called plate tectonics.
    C) Its atmosphere consists primarily of nitrogen and oxygen.
    D) It has an average density of 1 gm/cm3.
    E) It has a magnetic field.

16. The demonstration of the motion of the spinning top in class is related to
    A) the rotation of the Earth.
    B) the revolution of the Earth around the Sun.
    C) the precession of the Earth's axis.
    D) the gravity of the Earth.
    E) None of the above.

17. The precession of the Earth's axis is caused by the gravitational pull of the
    A) Moon acting on a spherical Earth.
    B) Sun acting on a spherical Earth.
    C) Sun and Moon acting on the oceans of the Earth.
    D) Sun and Moon acting on the equatorial bulge of the Earth.
    E) None of the above.

18. A critical test which demonstrates that the Earth rotates upon an axis is the observed behavior of
    A) the Coriolis effect.
    B) the apparent daily motion of the stars.
    C) sundials.
    D) eclipses of the Moon.
    E) the changing phases of the Moon.

19. The Coriolis effect on the Earth is caused by the
    A) atmosphere of the Earth.
    B) gravity of the Earth.
    C) tidal force of the Moon upon the Earth.
    D) rotation of the Earth.
    E) spherical shape of the Earth.

20. Scientists can deduce the structure of the interior of the Earth by
    A) drilling very deep holes.
    B) observing perturbations of the Moon's orbit.
    C) observing the variation of the rotation of the Earth.
    D) mapping seismic waves that emanate from earthquakes.
    E) none of the above.

21. During one year the Earth varies in distance from the Sun by about 3%. We can be sure that this is NOT the cause of the changing seasons because
    A) the seasons vary by much more than 3%.
    B) distance has no effect on the heat received from the Sun.
    C) it is summer north of the equator at the same time it is winter south of the equator.
    D) the Earth rotates 365 times faster than it revolves.
    E) None of the above are sufficient arguments.

22. Most earthquakes are caused, directly or indirectly, by
    A) volcanos erupting.   B) tides.   C) rotation of the Earth.
    D) slow drifting of large continental plates.   E) friction between the oceans and the land beneath them.

23. If the axis of rotation of the Earth were perpendicular to the plane of its orbit, which of the following would cease to occur?
    A) Eclipses of the Moon.   B) Parallax of the stars.   C) Eclipses of the Sun.
    D) The Coriolis effect.   E) Changing of the seasons.

24. Which of the following observed phenomena gives a compelling argument that the shape of the Earth is a sphere?
    A) Ships appear to vanish over the horizon.
    B) The sky appears to turn around us.
    C) The altitude of the north star increases as you travel north
    D) During a lunar eclipse the Earth's shadow is circular.
    E) During all lunar eclipses the Earth's shadow is circular.

25. On which of the following does the Coriolis effect operate?
    A) Winds blowing around high and low pressure systems.
    B) Ocean currents.
    C) Artillery projectiles.
    D) Rocket launched space vehicles.
    E) All of the above.

Chapter 5

1. The Moon probably formed when
    A) it was captured from Venus early in the system's history.
    B) it condensed from ices in the Earth's early atmosphere.
    C) matter was blasted out of the Earth by a huge impacting planetesimal.
    D) its matter was ejected in a huge series of volcanic eruptions.
    E) None of the above make any sense.

2. One reason the Moon has no atmosphere is because
    A) the Earth's gravity has stripped it off.
    B) the Sun's gravity has stripped it off.
    C) the Moon's gravity is too weak to hold it.
    D) the Moon's gravity is so strong that gas can't escape from the surface rock.
    E) None of the above.

3. The Lunar Mare
    A) are large, circular dark areas which form the "man-in-the-moon".
    B) are smooth, ancient lava flows.
    C) were formed by the impact of enormous asteroids.
    D) are named "seas" because they looked like water to ancient astronomers.
    E) All of the above.

4. The Moon
    A) does not rotate.
    B) rotates keeping the same face to the Earth.
    C) rotates so that its spin rate matches its orbital rate around the Earth.
    D) rotates three times for each orbit of the Earth.
    E) Only B) and C).

5. If the Moon were new tonight, when is the earliest a lunar eclipse could occur?
    A) tonight   B) tomorrow   C) two weeks off   D) a month off
    E) It is impossible to tell from the available information.

6. The most widely accepted theory at this time for the origin of the Moon is that it was born from
    A) the break up of the rapidly spinning young Earth.
    B) the capture by the Earth of a stray planetesimal.
    C) a huge impact, blasting matter out of the Earth and condensing into the Moon.
    D) second swarm of planetesimals condensing in orbit around the Earth.
    E) an enormous volcanic eruption on the Earth that blasted gas and debris into space.

7. Lunar rays are
    A) bright spots seen inside some craters.
    B) long narrow light-colored streaks of pulverized rock forming a radial pattern around some craters.
    C) bright flashes from otherwise inactive volcanic peaks seen when the Moon is full.
    D) bright flashes seen during a lunar eclipse.
    E) cracks in the lunar crust that radiate away from some craters.

8. Lunar rilles are
    A) narrow canyons.
    B) peculiar square craters seen in some mare.
    C) narrow bright lines that form a radial pattern around some craters.
    D) the raised ridges of ancient craters.
    E) mountain peaks at the center of some volcanic craters.

9. The lunar highlands are
    A) lighter colored than the dark mare basins.
    B) more heavily cratered than the Mare.
    C) composed of less dense rock than the mare.
    D) older than the mare.
    E) all of the above.

10. Most lunar craters were formed by
    A) impact of solid objects that blasted holes in the Moon's crust.
    B) volcanic eruptions triggered by eclipses.
    C) plate tectonic motions that cause the surface to collapse in round holes.
    D) the tidal force of the Earth drawing hot material from the lunar core to the surface where it explodes as it comes in contact with the cold temperature of space.
    E) convection of hot material in the lunar interior that sends bubbles to the surface that burst and form a hole.

11. One reason for rejecting the theory that the Moon formed from material spun off the Earth is that
    A) lunar rocks have a different composition than terrestrial rocks.
    B) no hole can be identified on the Earth from where the Moon broke off.
    C) lunar rocks are much older than 4.5 billion years.
    D) the Moon is nearly pure iron: It would therefore have to have formed from material in the earth's core.
    E) All of the above are important reasons to reject the theory.

12. A total eclipse of the Sun is due on October 10th. The next total eclipse of the Sun will probably occur
    A) October 10 the following year.   B) October 17.   C) October 24.
    D) January 10 the following year.   E) April 10 the following year.

13. What is the Moon's phase when a total lunar eclipse occurs.
    A) New.   B) First quarter.   C) Full.   D) third quarter.
    E) a lunar eclipse can happen at any lunar phase.

14. What is the minimum time that must elapse between a solar and a lunar eclipse?
    A) Several hours.   B) About one week.   C) About two weeks.
    D) About one month.   E) About six months.

15. The instructor was walking around the table with her nose pointing toward the center of the table during one lecture. She was demonstrating
    A) the revolution of the Earth around the Sun
    B) the synchronous rotation of the Moon.
    C) the precession of the Moon's orbit.
    D) Newton's law of universal gravitation.
    E) her keen sense of gauging the mood of the class.

16. Before the Apollo landings on the Moon, the lunar maria were known to be younger than the highlands because they
    A) have fewer craters.   B) have more craters.   C) are darker in color.
    D) are lighter in color.   E) used to be flooded with water.

17. Which of the following statements about the Moon is incorrect?
    A) It was once much closer to the Earth.
    B) It keeps the same face toward the Earth.
    C) It has no atmosphere.
    D) Its rocks have virtually no embedded water.
    E) It was most likely formed from material flung out by a rapidly rotating proto-Earth.

18. Eclipses do not occur each month because
    A) the angular diameter of the Moon varies.
    B) the Moon is never in the ecliptic.
    C) the Earth's axis is tilted to the orbital plane.
    D) the Moon's orbit is tilted from the orbital plane of the Earth.
    E) the sky is sometimes cloudy.

19. Solar eclipses are sometimes total and sometimes annular because
    A) the Moon is sometimes bigger (in angular diameter) and sometimes smaller than the Sun.
    B) the Moon is sometimes full and sometimes new.
    C) the Moon is sometimes in the ecliptic and sometimes off.
    D) the Moon is sometimes below the plane of the Earth's orbit and sometimes above.
    E) the Sun sometimes contracts and sometimes expands.

20. The maria of the moon are thought to have originated as
    A) bodies of water which are now dried up.
    B) uplifted plains (highlands).
    C) lava flows from huge volcanoes.
    D) areas eroded by wind before the Moon lost its atmosphere.
    E) lava flows that flooded giant impact craters.

21. The ocean tides raised by the Sun and the Moon on the Earth reinforce each other when
    A) the phase of the Moon is first or third quarter.
    B) the phase of the Moon is new or full.
    C) the Earth is closest to the Sun.
    D) the Moon is closest to the Earth.
    E) None of the above.

22. Eclipses of the Sun and the Moon do NOT occur every month because the
    A) Earth's axis of rotation is inclined to its orbital plane.
    B) Earth's orbit is not a circle.
    C) Moon's orbit is not a circle.
    D) Moon's orbit is tilted with respect to the Earth's orbit.
    E) Moon's synodic period is longer than its orbital period.

23. At the beach we see the tide coming in, and then going out. That is actually caused by the
    A) rotation of the Earth.
    B) orbital motion of the Earth around the Sun.
    C) orbital motion of the Moon around the Earth.
    D) rotation of the Moon.
    E) winds.

24. The synodic period of the Moon is the period of its phases. That period is longer than its true orbital period because
    A) the Earth is moving around the Sun.
    B) the orbit of the Moon is not a circle.
    C) the Moon rotates on its own axis.
    D) tides have slowed the lunar rotation.
    E) the Sun is moving through space.

25. Astronauts living at a future base on the Moon would find that one or more of the following effects would not occur there. Which would NOT occur on the Moon?
    A) Parallax of the stars.
    B) The Coriolis effect.
    C) Sunrise and sunset.
    D) Rising and setting of the Earth.
    E) None of the above would happen there.

26. One hemisphere of the Moon constantly faces the Earth, and the other is never seen. This occurs because the
    A) Moon does not rotate on an axis like the Earth does.
    B) Moon's rotation period is equal to its orbital period.
    C) Moon's rotation period is equal to its synodic period.
    D) Moon's axis of rotation points toward the Earth.
    E) Moon rotates half as fast as its orbital angular speed.

27. The synchronous rotation of the Moon is a direct result of
    A) Kepler's third law.   B) Kepler's second law.   C) an extraordinary coincidence.
    D) tidal forces exerted on it by the Earth.   E) unknown causes.

28. An eclipse of the Moon occurs when the
    A) Earth gets inside the shadow of the Moon.   B) Moon gets inside the shadow of the Earth.
    C) Moon gets between the Earth and the Sun.   D) Moon reaches its NEW phase.
    E) Moon reaches quadrature.

29. People see many more eclipses of the Moon than eclipses of the Sun in their lives. This occurs because
    A) lunar eclipses occur far more often than solar eclipses.
    B) lunar eclipses occur at night.
    C) solar eclipses can occur only during the daytime.
    D) one whole hemisphere of Earth views every lunar eclipse.
    E) all of the above are reasons for this fact.

30. If the Moon were totally eclipsed for us, an astronaut on the Moon, facing us, would see
    A) a total eclipse of the Sun.   B) a total eclipse of the Earth.
    C) nothing unusual.   D) much longer shadows of lunar mountains.
    E) a large dark shadow moving across the surface of the Earth.

31. If an astronaut on the Moon released a small object like a golf ball, it would
    A) fall toward the Earth.   B) fall toward the Moon.   C) fall toward the Sun.
    D) not fall because there is no gravity there.   E) be impossible to predict what it would do.

32. The FULL Moon must always
    A) appear only in the eastern sky.
    B) appear only in the western sky.
    C) rise at or very near the time that the Sun sets.
    D) pass directly over the observer's head during the night.
    E) be visible in the daytime sky.

33. Ancient cultures could predict the occurrence of eclipses of the Sun by making use of
   A) the theory of gravitation.   B) Kepler's first law.   C) Kepler's second law.
   D) Kepler's third law.   E) The Saros cycle.

34. Astronauts walking on the surface of the Moon do not float off into space because
   A) the Moon's gravity holds them down.
   B) air pressure on the Moon holds them down.
   C) they are tethered to their ship by ropes.
   D) the Earth's gravity holds them down.
   E) they wear heavy boots.

35. Astronauts on the Moon looking at the Earth would see each of the following effects except one. Which of the following would NOT happen?
   A) The Earth would appear 4 times larger than the Moon did.
   B) The Earth would appear to rotate.
   C) The Earth would rise in the east and set in the west.
   D) The Earth would be stationary in the sky and never move.
   E) The Earth would display the same set of phases that the Moon displays each month.

36. Lunar eclipses are observed to last about 2 hours, while solar eclipses are observed to last about 2 minutes. The explanation for that difference is that the
   A) Moon's shadow moves, but the Earth's shadow does not.
   B) Moon moves much faster at new phase than at full phase.
   C) Earth's rotation speed is 1/2 that of the lunar shadow.
   D) Sun is very much larger than the Moon.
   E) Earth's shadow is larger than the Moon, but the Moon's shadow is smaller than the Earth.

37. Eclipses of the Sun and Moon do NOT always occur at the same time of the year (i.e. the same month) because the
   A) Earth moves around the Sun.
   B) Moon moves around the Earth.
   C) Moon's orbital plane slowly rotates.
   D) the time it takes for the Earth to orbit the Sun is not exactly 12 months.
   E) Moon's orbital plane is tilted with respect to the Earth's orbital plane.

38. Astronauts at a permanent lunar base would notice that the Earth
   A) rises on the east horizon and sets on the west horizon.
   B) rises on the west horizon and sets on the east horizon.
   C) never rises, never sets, and never moves.
   D) is above the horizon for 2 weeks and below for 2 weeks.
   E) takes one lunar sidereal period to go around the Moon.

39. Ancient astronomers were able to predict the occurrence of eclipses of the Sun and Moon because
   A) they knew the lunar orbital period accurately.
   B) they knew the length of the cycle of lunar phases accurately.
   C) all eclipses occur in regular repeating cycles.
   D) they developed a nearly correct theory of orbits.
   E) eclipses occurred more frequently then than now.

40. The apparent diameter of the Moon varies as it moves on the sky around the Earth. This is caused by the fact that the
- A) Moon's orbit is elliptical.
- B) Moon's size is distort by gravitational effects of the Sun.
- C) Moon expands and contracts as it moves in orbit.
- D) tides of the Earth upon the Moon.
- E) orbit of the Moon is unstable.

41. Ancient astronomers knew that the Moon shines by reflecting sunlight. They deduced this fact from the
- A) color of the Moon.   B) phases of the Moon.   C) motion of the Moon.
- D) tides.   E) brightness of the Moon.

42. The ocean tides on the Earth are responsible for
- A) causing the Earth to rotate.
- B) making the Earth slightly bulged at its equator.
- C) causing a change in direction of Earth's rotation axis.
- D) moderating the seasonal variations.
- E) slowing the speed of the rotation of the Earth.

43. The ultimate fate of the Earth and Moon (and any other pair of orbiting astronomical bodies where tides are present) is
- A) collision of the two objects.
- B) synchronous rotation of the two objects.
- C) causing the orbit to become elliptical.
- D) breakup of the orbiting pair and escape.
- E) tilting of the rotation axes of the two bodies.

44. Due to the orbital motion of the Moon, successive high tides raised by the Moon occur at intervals of
- A) exactly 12 hours.   B) slightly less than 12 hours.   C) slightly more than 12 hours.
- D) 24 hours.   E) lunar orbital motion has no effect on times of high tide.

Use the following code to describe what would happen to the ocean tides if the different circumstances described in each statement prevailed.
- A) Tides would cease to occur.
- B) Observed tides would become larger than they are now.
- C) Observed tides would become smaller than they are now.
- D) No change would occur to the presently observed tides.

45. If the Earth did not have a moon.
46. If the Moon were twice its present distance.
47. If the period of Earth's rotation were the same as the orbital period of the Moon.

ESSAY 4

1. We have leap years because
    A) every four years the Earth changes its direction in its orbit.
    B) we need to adjust clocks for the slow down of the Earth's rotation rate.
    C) the year is 365.25 days long, not an even 365 days.
    D) the month is not exactly 30 days long.
    E) the week has 7 days not 7.25 days.

2. The solar day is
    A) the time from sunrise to sunrise.
    B) the time from star-rise to star-rise.
    C) longer than the sidereal day.
    D) equal to 23 hours 56 minutes.
    E) both A and C.

3. The sidereal day is
    A) the time interval between successive crossings of the meridian by a star.
    B) shorter than the apparent solar day.
    C) equal to 24 hours.
    D) both A and B.
    E) both A and C.

4. Which of the following years will not be a leap year?
    A) 1996   B) 2000   C) 2004   D) 2100   E) None of the above.

5. The time interval for the Moon to complete a cycle of its phases is
    A) the sidereal month.   B) the synodic month.   C) about 29.5 days.
    D) Both A and C.   E) Both B and C.

Chapter 6

1. The age of the Solar System is about ____ years.
   A) 45,000   B) 4.5 million   C) 4.5 billion   D) 45 trillion   E) 4500

2. How can we deduce the Solar System's age?
   A) From the amount of hydrogen in Earth rocks.
   B) From the ratio of hydrogen in the Earth's atmosphere compared with that in its crust.
   C) From the ratio of radioactive materials in samples of old rocks.
   D) From how long it takes light to cross the Solar System.
   E) From the speed with which distant galaxies move.

3. What is meant by the solar nebula?
   A) A cloud of gas around the outer edges of the Solar System.
   B) Another name for the Sun's outer atmosphere.
   C) Another name for our galaxy, the Milky Way.
   D) The disk of gas from which the Sun and planets formed.
   E) Gas ejected from the Sun which fills the inner Solar System.

4. The Oort Cloud is
   A) the source of comets.
   B) the source of rocky asteroids.
   C) the source of the satellites of Jupiter.
   D) another name for the clouds of Venus.   E) none of the above.

5. Bode's law involves
   A) a planet's mass.   B) the distance to nearby stars.   C) a planet's distance from the Sun.
   D) the spectral classes.   E) none of the above.

6. The flat shape of the Solar System results from
   A) a collision of the early system with another cloud that squashed it.
   B) intense magnetic fields in the early Solar System.
   C) both A) and B).
   D) rotation of the original cloud from which it formed.
   E) the statement is false. The system of the planets is not flattened.

7. The terrestrial planets are rocky because
   A) the Sun's gravity drew primarily heavy elements into the inner part of the early Solar System.
   B) the Sun converted all the hydrogen and helium in the inner Solar System into iron and nickel.
   C) once planetesimals formed, the rocky ones drifted inward and the icy ones moved outward in the Solar System.
   D) only rocky material was able to condense in the hot inner part of the early solar nebula.
   E) the statement is misleading in that the terrestrial planets are not appreciably more rocky than Jupiter or Saturn.

8. The solar nebula is
   A) a cloud of gas in the corona.
   B) the place where comet nuclei are now found.
   C) another name for a prominence.
   D) a name for the disk of dust and gas from which the planets formed.
   E) none of the above.

9. The cratered surfaces on many planets and satellites are evidence that
    A) volcanic activity was common in the early Solar System.
    B) aliens waged a nuclear war in the early Solar System.
    C) gravity was much stronger in the past than now.
    D) remnant planetesimals and their fragments bombarded the surfaces.
    E) The statement is misleading. Very few solid bodies in the Solar System show craters.

10. In using Bode's law, suppose that you began 0,4, instead of 0, 3 but then calculated exactly as in the original law. How far would the Earth be from the Sun?
    A) .8 AU   B) 8 AU   C) 12 AU   D) 1.2 AU   E) None of the above.

11. Bode's Law describes
    A) a planet's radius and escape velocity.   B) its mass and orbital velocity.
    C) the number of satellites of a planet.   D) the size of a planet's rings.
    E) none of the above

12. The reason that there are two main types of planets is that
    A) the Sun gravity drew iron and silicate chunks close to it as the planets formed.
    B) hydrogen and helium, being light gases, drifted to the outer parts of the Solar System where the outer planets condensed.
    C) the Sun's magnetic field drew iron and silicates inward as planets formed.
    D) the Sun's heat prevented ices and gases condensing near it.
    E) None of the above

13. The names of the planets in order of their <u>usual</u> distance from the Sun are
    A) Mercury, Venus, Earth, Jupiter, Mars, Neptune, Uranus, Pluto.
    B) Venus, Mercury, Earth, Mars, Jupiter, Saturn, Uranus, Neptune, Pluto.
    C) Venus, Mercury, Earth, Mars, Jupiter, Saturn, Neptune, Uranus, Pluto.
    D) Mercury, Mars, Venus, Earth, Saturn, Jupiter, Neptune, Uranus, Pluto.
    E) Mercury, Venus, Earth, Mars, Jupiter, Saturn, Uranus, Neptune, Pluto.

14 Which statement below concerning a comparison between the Jovian planets and the terrestrial planets is not true?
    A) The Jovian planets have larger diameters.
    B) The Jovian planets have higher densities.
    C) The Jovian planets have shorter rotation periods.
    D) The Jovian planets have greater masses.
    E) The Jovian planets have more satellites.

15. Which of the following statements about the formation of the planets is incorrect?
    A) The solar nebula resembled a rotating disk.
    B) Random collisions among the rocky grains led to the formation of planetesimals.
    C) The planetesimals grew in size through gravitational accretion.
    D) The terrestrial planets are small and rocky, in comparison with the Jovian planets, because hydrogen and helium could not condense in the inner part of the solar nebula.
    E) None of the above.

Chapter 7
1. The Venusian clouds are made primarily of
    A) water.   B) carbon dioxide.   C) sodium chloride.   D) iron sulfide.   E) sulfuric acid.

2. Differentiation refers to
    A) planets forming two types around the Sun.
    B) the creation of the primordial background radiation.
    C) the settling of heavy elements - like iron - to the center of an object.
    D) the break up of the Earth's crust into plates that move.
    E) none of the above.

3. The large number of craters seen on most solid planetary surfaces shows
    A) they experienced an intense meteoritic bombardment near the end of their formation.
    B) they underwent intense volcanic eruptions as they cooled.
    C) plate tectonics completely wiped out their original surface leaving only holes.
    D) planets experienced intense lightning storms earlier in their history.
    E) none of the above.

4. The atmosphere of Mars is mostly
    A) hydrogen.   B) methane.   C) nitrogen.   D) CO_2.   E) It has no atmosphere.

5. Why do we think the climate of Mars has changed?
    A) Old river beds exist, but no water flows there today.
    B) Fossil trees show it was once hot and not so dry.
    C) Photographs taken in 1950 show it was once green.
    D) Ancient Chinese records say it looked blue-green like the Earth.
    E) None of the above.

6. The high temperature on the surface of Venus is caused by
    A) its intense volcanic activity.
    B) tidal forces generated by its small but dense moon.
    C) the extreme radioactivity of its atmosphere.
    D) trapping of solar energy by the carbon dioxide in its atmosphere.
    E) none of the above. Venus isn't so hot as all that.

7. Astronomers are convinced that Mars used to have a lot of water because
    A) huge subsurface deposits of ice have been seen with x-ray telescopes.
    B) each martian summer large lakes form as the polar caps melt.
    C) there is an huge amount of water vapor in the dense martian clouds.
    D) the surface has many canyons that appear to have been cut by running water.
    E) The statement is false. Mars appears to have always been extremely dry.

8. Which of the following features is not found on Mars?
    A) deserts.   B) oceans.   C) volcanoes.   D) polar caps.   E) an atmosphere.

Identify the planet and its features. Choices may be used more than once or not at all.
    A) Venus   B) Mars   C) Mercury   D) Earth   E) not applicable to any of the objects
9. A single large moon
10. Most massive terrestrial planet
11. No atmosphere
12. Polar caps of carbon dioxide
13. Dense hydrogen/methane atmosphere
14. Planet nearest the Sun
15. Hottest average surface temperature found on any terrestrial planet
16. Craters are about the only surface features seen on this body.
17. Nitrogen rich atmosphere

18. In addition to the Earth, liquid water presently exists on the surface of
    A) the Moon.   B) Mercury.   C) Venus.   D) Mars.   E) Nowhere in the solar system.

19. The surface of Mercury is most similar to that of
    A) the Moon.   B) the Earth.   C) Mars.   D) Venus.   E) Jupiter.

20. Which of the following statements about Venus is incorrect?
    A) Its atmosphere contains carbon dioxide.
    B) It has an atmosphere that is much denser than the Earth's.
    C) It has a surface temperature that is much higher than the Earth's.
    D) It has volcanoes.
    E) It has a strong magnetic field.

21. On the surface of Mars we observe
    A) giant volcanoes.   B) polar caps.   C) vast canyons.
    D) dry riverbeds.   E) all of the above.

22. The atmosphere of Mars and Venus are similar in that they
    A) both have about the same temperature.
    B) both have about the same density.
    C) are both mainly composed of carbon dioxide.
    D) All of the above.
    E) None of the above.

23. If we list the terrestrial planets in the order of increasing amount of atmosphere, the list should read
    A) Mercury, Venus, Earth, Mars.
    B) Mercury, Mars, Earth, Venus.
    C) Mercury, Earth, Mars, Venus.
    D) Mars, Mercury, Earth, Venus.
    E) Mercury, Mars, Venus, Earth.

Chapter 8
1. The rings of Saturn are probably made of
    A) hot gas bound to the planet by gravity and inside Roche's limit.
    B) chunks of rock many miles in diameter captured from the asteroid belt.
    C) an immense solid disk of ice partially melted at Cassini's division by heat generated by Saturn.
    D) numerous small icy pieces, yards to inches in diameter, each moving in its own orbit.
    E) none of the above.

2. Most of the material in Jupiter is
    A) silicates.   B) iron.   C) water.   D) helium.   E) none of the above.

Identify the planet and its features. Choices may be used more than once or not at all.
A) Jupiter   B) Saturn   C) Uranus   D) Pluto   E) applicable to more than one.
    3. Composed mainly of ice and rock
    4. Most massive jovian planet
    5. Atmosphere rich in hydrogen and its compounds such as methane
    6. Has a set of rings.
    7. Has a uniform pale blue color caused by the methane in its atmosphere.
    8. Io is one of its moons.
    9. Its orbit crosses Neptune's.
    10. Winds in its atmosphere create huge vortices such as the great red spot.
    11. Has a rocky/iron core similar in size to the Earth.

12. The rings seen around the Jovian planets lie
    A) inside the planet's upper atmosphere.
    B) inside the planet's Roche Limit.
    C) outside the planet's Roche limit.
    D) at the place where the planet's and Sun's gravity cancel out exactly.
    E) none of the above.

13. Jupiter has a large equatorial bulge because
    A) it has such a strong magnetic field.
    B) it is so rich in hydrogen.
    C) of tidal forces exerted by its satellites.
    D) it rotates so rapidly.   E) none of the above.

14. The odd tilt to Uranus's rotation axis may have been caused by
    A) the asteroid Gaspra passing so close to Uranus that its gravity pulled it over.
    B) a collision with a large planetesimal during its formation.
    C) the Sun's gravity pulling it over.
    D) Jupiter's gravity.
    E) the event that tossed Pluto out of its system of moons.

15. Io is
    A) noted for its sulfur volcanoes.   B) a satellite of Neptune.   C) comparable in size to Mercury.
    D) a garish red and yellow color.   E) All the above except B).

Match the planet with its property or feature. Use each choice only once.

    16. Pluto   A) AT THIS TIME furthest from Sun
    17. Uranus   B) Planet with the lowest density
    18. Neptune   C) strongly marked with cloud belts and zones
    19. Saturn   D) orbits of its moons are highly tilted (about 90°)
    20. Jupiter   E) Icy body with thin methane atmosphere.

21. The reason planetary rings are always so close to the body of the planet is
    A) matter in them is boiled out of the planet's atmosphere.
    B) the planet's gravity is stronger there and can help hold them together.
    C) the planet's gravity is weakest there and prevents them from clotting up.
    D) the planet's gravity is large enough there to disrupt medium size bodies and keep the pieces spread out.
    E) none of the above

In the following, match the object with the description. Use each choice only once.
A) Titan   B) Ceres   C) Uranus   D) Jupiter   E) Io

22. Larger than Mercury and with an atmosphere.
23. Rocky or iron body. Diameter about 1000 km.
24. This planet may have suffered a major impact at birth that tipped its rotation axis.
25. Active sulfur erupting volcanos.
26. This body has a ring, red spot, and is bigger than all the other planets put together.

27. Most of the material in Jupiter is
    A) silicates.   B) iron.   C) water.   D) nitrogen.   E) none of the above are correct.

28. The first planet to be discovered by a mathematical prediction was
    A) Jupiter.   B) Saturn.   C) Uranus.   D) Neptune.   E) Pluto.

29. The planet whose axis of rotation is tilted by about 90 degrees is
    A) Jupiter.   B) Saturn.   C) Uranus.   D) Neptune.   E) Venus.

30. Which of the following statements does not describe Jupiter?
    A) It is the largest planet in the solar system.
    B) It has a stormy atmosphere.
    C) It emits radio waves.
    D) Jupiter and its Galilean satellites resemble a miniature solar system.
    E) All of them correctly describe Jupiter.

31. Which of the following statements about Saturn is incorrect?
    A) It is composed primarily of molecular hydrogen and helium.
    B) Its magnetic field is stronger than the Earth's.
    C) Its rings consist of thousands of ringlets.
    D) Its satellite, Titan, has a thin atmosphere of CO_2.
    E) None of the above.

32. Which of the following satellites has a dense atmosphere of N_2?
    A) Io   B) Titan   C) Enceladus   D) Triton   E) None of the above.

33. The very strong magnetic field of Jupiter (as compared to Earth's) is due to
    A) Jupiter's more rapid rotation.
    B) Jupiter's large region of liquid metallic hydrogen.
    C) Jupiter's stormy atmosphere.
    D) All of the above.
    E) Both A and B.

34. Which of the following statements does not apply to Saturn.
    A) It is noticeably bigger at its equator.
    B) Its magnetic field is stronger than the Earth's.
    C) Its internal structure is similar to that of Jupiter.
    D) Its atmosphere consists primarily of molecular hydrogen and helium.
    E) All of the above apply to Saturn.

35. Which of the following statements about the rings of Saturn is incorrect?
    A) The rings lie in the equatorial plane of Saturn.
    B) The rings consist of thousands of ringlets.
    C) The ring particles are rocks coated with ice.
    D) The ring particles range in diameter from about 0.01 cm to about 100 feet.
    E) The particles in the different rings orbit Saturn with the same period.

36. The planet with a great dark blue spot is
    A) Jupiter   B) Saturn   C) Uranus   D) Neptune   E) Pluto

37. The two objects that orbit each other with the same face toward each other are
    A) Pluto and Charon.   B) Neptune and Triton.   C) Saturn and Titan.
    D) Jupiter and Io.   E) Earth and Moon.

38. A distinctive feature that sets Triton apart from other large moons is
    A) its retrograde orbital motion.
    B) its size.
    C) the composition of its interior.
    D) its density.
    E) none of the above.

39. Which statement below concerning the Jovian planets is incorrect?
    A) The Jovian planets are composed primarily of hydrogen and helium.
    B) The Jovian planets have lower densities than terrestrial planets.
    C) The Jovian planets have longer sidereal periods than terrestrial planets.
    D) The Jovian planets have more satellites than terrestrial planets.
    E) None of the above.

40. Which of the following objects is not a moon of Jupiter?
    A) Mimas   B) Io   C) Ganymede   D) Europa   E) Callisto

Solar System - General

Match the planet with its property or description. Choices may be used more than once or not at all.
A) Jupiter. B) Venus. C) Mars. D) Pluto E) Uranus.
1. Planet with methane frost on its icy surface.
2. Planet with carbon dioxide polar caps.
3. Planet closest in size to the Earth.
4. Planet with no moon.
5. Planet with dense carbon dioxide atmosphere.
6. Planet with weirdly tilted rotation axis - the result of impact?

Match the body with its surface or atmospheric features. Choices may be used more than once or not at all.
7. Sulfur volcanoes   A) Mars
8. Carbon dioxide atmosphere   B) Jupiter
9. Solid surface of frozen methane ice   C) Io
10. Prominent cloud belts   D) Ceres
11. A thick atmosphere rich in hydrogen E) Pluto

Why do we see so few craters on the Earth compared to the Moon?
A) Plate tectonics has altered the Earth's crust, obliterating them.
B) The Moon was more intensely bombarded by asteroids.
C) The Moon is more volcanically active than the Earth.
D) The Moon formed long before the Earth.
E) The Moon formed in the asteroid belt and was captured later.

Match Planet/satellite and features. Choices may be used more than once or not at all.
A) Mercury B) Io C) Earth D) Venus E) Mars.
13. Volcanoes of liquid sulfur.
14. Heavily cratered. May have lost original surface in huge impact.
15. Sand Dunes, old, empty river beds.
16. Extensive plate tectonics. Rifting and currently active volcanoes.
17. Immense surface lava flows. Some folded mountains. carbon dioxide atmosphere.

Planetesimals play an important role in
A) explaining the craters on the surface of the terrestrial planets.
B) creating gaps in planetary rings.
C) certain religious ceremonies of the Klingons.
D) the conversion of dust and gas in the solar nebula into planets.
E) both A) and D).

Which planet has a surface very like that of our Moon?
A) Mercury. B) Venus. C) Mars. Jupiter. E) Uranus.

Why are the terrestrial planets so much smaller than the jovian ones?
A) The mass that should have gone into them ended up in their moons.
B) They are formed from highly compressible material such as hydrogen and helium so they could be squeezed to a tiny size.
C) Near the Sun, only hard to melt substances - which are rare compared to hydrogen - could condense. Thus, there was less material to build them.
D) They spin so fast they flung off most of their original matter which has ended up in the comet cloud.
E) The Sun has pulled material off of them.

Match the planet/astronomical object with its property.
- 21. Mars.
- 22. Mercury
- 23. Venus
- 24. Earth
- 25. Pluto

A) Thin methane atmosphere.
B) No atmosphere.
C) Dense carbon dioxide atmosphere. Sulfuric acid clouds.
D) Abundant liquid water on surface.
E) thin carbon dioxide atmosphere and "dry ice" polar caps.

26. The greenhouse effect on a planet causes
    A) the formation of water.
    B) evolution of living material.
    C) the atmosphere to evaporate away.
    D) higher surface temperatures than Sunlight alone makes.
    E) lower surface temperatures than sunlight alone makes.

27. The cause of the greenhouse effect on a planet is
    A) rapid rotation of the planet.
    B) excess ultraviolet absorption by the atmosphere.
    C) trapping of infrared absorption by the atmosphere.
    D) reflection of ultraviolet by the atmosphere.
    E) reflection of infrared by the atmosphere.

28. The large dark regions on our Moon (called maria) are thought to be the result of
    A) impacts by huge meteoric masses.
    B) gigantic lava flows from long ago.
    C) atmospheric deposits over billions of years.
    D) rapid rotation of the young Moon.
    E) chemical erosion over billions of years.

29. Pictures and other data of the surfaces of planets and their Moons gathered by space probes give evidence that the evolution of the early Solar System was dominated by
    A) intense impact cratering.   B) solar radiation.   C) a long period of quiescence.
    D) chemical processes.   E) thermal processes.

30. Compared to its neighboring planets, Mercury, Venus, and Mars, the surface of the Earth is relatively young. This youthful appearance results from
    A) the Earth being the most recently formed of these planets.
    B) the Earth having the largest Moon of all of these planets.
    C) tectonic activity still shaping the surface of the Earth.
    D) the Earth being the only one of these planets with an atmosphere.
    E) no impact cratering ever occurring on the Earth.

31. Chemical evidence suggests that the atmospheres of the inner planets formed by
    A) accretion of gas from the Sun.
    B) accretion of gas from space as they condensed.
    C) evaporation of surface materials.
    D) evolution of living materials.
    E) volcanic releases of internal gasses.

32. A remarkable discovery about the rings of Saturn made by the Voyager probes was that the rings
    A) are circular.   B) are made of tiny particles.   C) orbit around the planet.
    D) are very thin.   E) consist of hundreds of separate rings.

33. The Voyager probes discovered that the innermost satellite of Jupiter (called Io) is very unusual because it has
   A) craters on its surface.   B) ice on its surface.   C) mountains on its surface.
   D) active volcanos on its surface.   E) a very non-spherical shape.

34. One effect of the Moon's gravity upon the Earth is to make
   A) the Earth's magnetic field.
   B) the Earth rotate.
   C) the oceans change their levels.
   D) the Earth's poles colder than the equator.
   E) nothing at all since it is too weak.

Suppose the Earth did NOT rotate, but everything else remained as it is now. Use the following code to describe what would happen to each of the phenomena listed below.
   A) no change.   B) change.   C) cease to occur.

35. Seasons in each of the hemispheres.
36. Sunrise and sunset at any location.
37. Coriolis effects.
38. Precession.
39. Phases of the Moon.

Suppose the axis of rotation of the Earth was perpendicular to the plane of its orbit, and not inclined by 23.5 degrees. Use the following code to describe the effect of that on each phenomenon.
   A) No change.   B) Change.   C) Cease to occur.

40. The phases of the Moon.
41. The number of hours between sunrise and sunset.
42. The height of high and low tides in the oceans.
43. The seasons in both hemispheres.
44. The duration of our year (orbital period of Earth).
45. The length of the cycle of lunar phases (the synodic period of the Moon).
46. Appearance and frequency of lunar eclipses.
47. Coriolis effects on the Earth's surface.

Chapter 9

1. The glow of a meteor is caused by
    A) reflected Sunlight.
    B) trapping of dust by the Earth's magnetic field.
    C) radioactive decay in the meteoritic matter.
    D) frictional heating as it moves through the atmosphere.
    E) none of the above.

2. Meteors are believed to originate from
    A) condensations in the solar wind.
    B) stray asteroidal fragments entering our atmosphere.
    C) the Earth encountering dust orbiting along the path of a comet.
    D) ice and frozen gas that falls into the Solar System from other galaxies.
    E) both B) and C).

3. Comet tails form because
    A) the Sun's gravity pulls material from the comet into a long plume.
    B) the Sun's magnetic field draws gases from the comet into a long filament.
    C) the Sun's radiation pressure and the solar wind push on gases evaporating from the comet and blow them into a plume.
    D) the Sun's gravity creates a gravitational lens which distorts the comet's image into a thin line of light that shifts as the Earth moves in its orbit.
    E) none of the above.

4. Comets are
    A) the remnants of huge terrestrial planet broken up by an explosion.
    B) small icy bodies which drop into the inner Solar System and are heated by the Sun.
    C) escaped satellites of the inner planets, especially Mercury and Venus.
    D) material captured from a passing star.
    E) none of the above.

5. When all of a comet's gases evaporate and it begins to disintegrate, it leaves behind material that causes
    A) meteor showers.   B) auroral activity.   C) solar flares.
    D) the asteroids.   E) none of the above.

6. Most meteors not associated with showers come from
    A) the asteroid belt.   B) particles ejected by Jupiter.   C) the Oort cloud.
    D) the Sun.   E) the solar wind.

7. The source of meteors is
    A) cometary debris.   B) asteroidal debris.   C) the solar wind.
    D) all the above.   E) only A) and B).

8. The asteroid belt lies between the orbits of
    A) Mars and Jupiter.   B) Jupiter and Saturn.   C) Saturn and Uranus.
    D) Uranus and Neptune.   E) Mercury and the Sun.

9. Comet tails always point toward the Sun because
    A) the Sun's gravity draws the material inward.
    B) the solar wind sucks them in.
    C) the gases are trapped in the Sun's magnetic field.
    D) none of the above are the correct explanation.
    E) the statement is rubbish. Comet tails point away from the Sun.

10. The fact that some asteroids are rocky while others are metallic (iron-rich) is explained by
    A) their forming near Jupiter, whose immense gravity drew the iron outward.
    B) the differences in their magnetic field. Ones with strong fields attracted lots of iron atoms.
    C) their being fragments of larger objects that had melted and formed iron cores.
    D) the Sun heating their surfaces and vaporizing the rock from some of the them.
    E) The statement is false. Asteroids are essentially all alike in their composition.

11. The direction a comet tail points is
    A) trailing behind it in its orbit.
    B) at right angles to its orbit.
    C) pointing ahead of it in its orbit.
    D) constantly changing because it always points toward Jupiter.
    E) none of the above.

12. The asteroids are probably
    A) the remnants of huge terrestrial planet broken up by an explosion.
    B) fragments and a few survivors of the planetesimals from which the Solar System formed.
    C) escaped satellites of the inner planets, especially Mercury and Venus.
    D) material captured from a passing star.
    E) none of the above are likely.

13. A meteor shower such as we have every August is caused by
    A) a large asteroid breaking up as it approaches earth.
    B) the Earth passing through the orbit of an old comet.
    C) a swarm of particles that orbits the Earth . The Moon's gravity disturbs them so that they fall into our atmosphere.
    D) a swarm of particles that orbits the Moon. The Earth's gravity disturbs them so that they fall into our atmosphere.
    E) eruptions from the surface of the Sun.

14. Which of the following statements about comets is incorrect?
    A) Their orbits are confined to the orbital plane of the planets.
    B) They have dust and gas tails.
    C) Matter is evaporated from them as they pass close to the Sun.
    D) They are appropriately described as dirty snow balls.
    E) They are located in a region that extends to about 150,000 AU from the Sun.

Chapter 10

1. The time interval between peaks of solar activity is about how long?
    A) 11 months   B) 5 years   C) 11 years   D) 12000 years   E) none of the above.

2. Sunspots are dark because
    A) they contain so much heavy material that light can't readily escape.
    B) the solar wind cools the surface locally.
    C) magnetic fields bring iron up from the core which blocks the light.
    D) local magnetic fields reduce convection below the surface and reduce the heat reaching the surface.
    E) none of the above.

3. 1991 was a good year for sunspots. The next time we can expect lots will be in
    A) 1992.   B) 2002.   C) 2013.   D) 2091.   E) we can't tell.

In the sketch of the Sun at the right, identify the following. (Choices may be used more than once or not at all).

4. A prominence
5. The corona
6. The chromosphere
7. The photosphere
8. The place you could see granulation

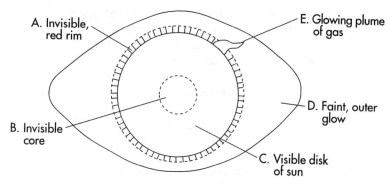

9. The Sun derives its energy from
    A) the conversion of mass into energy.
    B) the fusion of hydrogen into helium.
    C) chemical reactions that convert hydrogen and oxygen into carbon, accompanied by the release of neutrinos.
    D) a steady gravitational contraction of its core.
    E) Both A) and B).

10. What keeps the Sun from collapsing under its own gravity?
    A) The intense magnetic fields in its core.
    B) The fact that its interior is liquid and therefore can not be compressed.
    C) The fact that its interior is mostly iron, giving it great strength.
    D) The outward force exerted by pressure of the gas in its hot interior.
    E) The forces generated by its extremely rapid rotation.

11. The Sun's radius is about how much bigger/smaller than the Earth's?
    A) About 5 times bigger.   B) About 5 times smaller.
    C) Their radii are almost exactly the same. That is why we can have eclipses.
    D) About 100 times larger than the Earth's.   E) About a million times larger than the Earth's.

12. What keeps the Sun's hot gas from streaming off into space and dissipating?
    A) Its strong magnetic field.
    B) Its gravitational attraction.
    C) The fact that its gas is mostly iron and is therefore too heavy to escape.
    D) The pressure exerted on it from outside by the gas in interplanetary space.
    E) The steady infall of meteoritic dust that pushes the gas inward.

13. Why are astronomers interested in solar neutrinos?
    A) They allow the measurement of the strength of magnetic fields in sunspots.
    B) They are produced by nuclear reactions in the Sun's core and therefore give information about processes deep in the Sun.
    C) They are a deadly radiation of massive particles that gradually destroys the Earth's crust.
    D) They show that the Sun is burning helium in its core.
    E) They show that the Sun's core is iron and that it is spinning rapidly, thereby creating the solar cycle.

Match the region in the Sun as indicated in the diagram with the following terms or phenomena. Choices may be used more than once or not at all.

14. Photosphere
15. Convection Zone
16. Corona
17. Chromosphere
18. Region where hydrogen is converted into helium

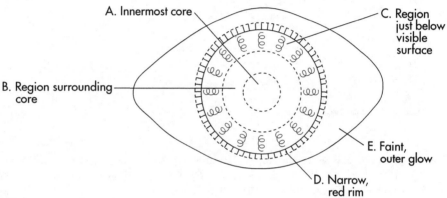

19. The Maunder minimum is
    A) a region between Saturn and Jupiter, with few if any, asteroids.
    B) a region in the Sun's atmosphere where the temperature is very low.
    C) the reason that sunspots are cool.
    D) a period in the 1600-1700's of few sunspots.
    E) none of the above.

20. Given that the Sun's mass is 2×10^{33} gm and its radius is 7×10^{10} cm, what is its density in gm/cm^3? Note: Volume of a sphere is $4\pi R^3/3$.
    A) 1.4 B) 14. C) .0025 D) 3.2×10^{23} E) None of the above are close.

21. The Sun is powered by the conversion of _____ into _____.
    A) hydrogen into helium   B) helium into carbon
    C) hydrogen and oxygen into water   D) gravity into mass   E) none of the above.

22. Hydrostatic equilibrium is the balance of
    A) pressure and nuclear forces.   B) magnetic and pressure forces.
    C) gravitational and pressure forces.
    D) nuclear energy production and radiation loss from the Sun's surface.
    E) None of the above.

23. The solar corona is normally visible at
    A) sunset. B) sunrise. C) new moon. D) a total lunar eclipse. E) a total solar eclipse.

24. A prominence is a/an
   A) arc of gas suspended by magnetic fields in the Sun's corona.
   B) a sudden brightening of gas near a sunspot.
   C) a sudden release of nuclear energy in the Sun's core.
   D) an abnormally large sunspot group.
   E) ignition of a pocket of helium gas in the convection zone.

25. Which of the following is the correct description of the p - p chain?

   A) $^1H + ^1H \longrightarrow {}^2He + e^+ + neutrino + Energy$
   $^2He + {}^1H \longrightarrow {}^3He + Energy$
   $^3He + {}^1H \longrightarrow {}^4He + Energy$

   B) $^1H + ^1H \longrightarrow {}^2H + e^+ + neutrino + Energy$
   $^2H + {}^1H \longrightarrow {}^3He + gamma\ ray + Energy$
   $^3He + {}^3He \longrightarrow {}^4He + {}^1H + {}^1H + Energy$

   C) $^1H + ^1H \longrightarrow {}^2H + Energy$
   $^2H + {}^1H \longrightarrow {}^3He + Energy$
   $^3He + {}^1H \longrightarrow {}^4He + Energy$

   D) $^1H + ^1H \longrightarrow {}^2H + e^+ + neutrino + Energy$
   $^2H + {}^1He \longrightarrow {}^3He + Energy$
   $^3He + {}^1H \longrightarrow {}^4He + Energy$

   E) none of the above.

26. The temperature, in degrees Kelvin, in the center of the Sun is closest to
   A) one billion.   B) one million.   C) fifteen million.
   D) one hundred thousand.   E) fifteen thousand.

27. Which of the following statements about the nuclear force is incorrect?
   A) It provides an attractive force between two protons.
   B) It provides an attractive force between a proton and a neutron.
   C) It provides an attractive force between two neutrons.
   D) It extends only over a very short range.
   E) None of the above.

28. Which of the following statements about the solar atmosphere is incorrect?
   A) Most of the visible light arises from the photosphere.
   B) The photosphere shows granulation.
   C) The hottest region of the solar atmosphere is the corona.
   D) The chromosphere appears red.
   E) None of the above.

29. Sunspots are
   A) regions where the gas is considerably cooler (by as much as 1500 K) than the surroundings.
   B) regions where the gas is considerably hotter than the surroundings.
   C) regions where the magnetic field is stronger.
   D) Both A and C.
   E) Both B and C.

30. Astronomers cannot measure the temperature of the central core of the Sun because
    A) black body laws fail at such high temperatures.
    B) all of the hydrogen has been converted to helium.
    C) the central core of the Sun is convective.
    D) we do not receive any radiation directly from the core.
    E) the central core is unstable.

31 Solar flares are thought to be caused by
    A) disrupting magnetic fields.   B) thermonuclear explosions.
    C) impacts from infalling asteroids.   D) hot coronal gas falling into the Sun. E) no known cause.

32. Astronomers think that the temperature of the solar CORONA is millions of degrees K; vastly hotter than its photosphere. The EVIDENCE for this belief is
    A) the black body radiation laws.
    B) the wavelength of maximum intensity is in the ultraviolet.
    C) all hydrogen in the corona has been converted to helium.
    D) emission lines show that the gas is highly ionized.
    E) there is no evidence since it is purely a theory.

Chapter 11

1. If a star's distance increases, the value of its apparent magnitude
   A) increases.
   B) decreases.
   C) is unaltered.
   D) you can't tell for sure. The apparent magnitude may do either.
   E) only absolute magnitude is related to distance.

2. A binary star pair have a period of 30 years and are separated by 15 AU. Their total mass is
   A) 2 M_{Sun} B) 1/2 M_{Sun} C) 4/15 M_{Sun}
   D) 15/4 M_{Sun} E) none of the above.

3. Two stars have the same temperature but one is much more luminous than the other.
   The brighter star must therefore be
   A) hotter. B) further away. C) less massive. D) smaller in radius. E) larger in radius.

4. The order of the spectral classes from cold to hot is
   A) O B A F G K M. B) A B F G K M O. C) M K G F A B O.
   D) I M A F R O G. E) A B F K G M O.

5. A star emits most strongly at 500 nm. Its temperature is
   A) 600 K. B) 6000 K. C) 60,000 K. D) 15,000 K. E) 1500 K.

6. A star has a luminosity 400 times that of the Sun. Its temperature is 12,000 compared to the Sun's 6,000.
   What is its radius in solar units?
   A) 5. B) 10. C) 0.2. D) 40. E) None of the above.

7. A binary star pair have a separation of 10 AU and orbital period of 5 years.
   What is their combined mass in units of the Sun's mass?
   A) 2. B) 4. C) 40. D) 0.5. E) 400.

8. What is the temperature of the star Sirius if it radiates most strongly at 300 nm?
   A) 9,000 K.   B) 10,000 K.   C) 3,000 K.   D) 30,000 K.   E) 300K.

9. What is the radius of the star Capella (in solar units) given that it is the same temperature as the Sun but is 100 times more luminous?
   A) 100.   B) 10,000.   C) 10.   D) 50.   E) The same radius.

10. The hottest of the normal stellar spectral classes is
    A) G.   B) M.   C) A.   D) B.   E) none of these.

11. A red giant's diameter is about how much bigger than the Sun's?
    A) twice as big.   B) half as big.   C) 10 times as big.
    D) 100 times as big.   E) a million times as big.

12. A star shows a spectral line at a wavelength of 600.3 nm that in the laboratory appears at 600 nm. How fast is it moving?
    A) 150 km/sec.   B) 15 km/sec.   C) 300 km/sec.   D) 30 km/sec.   E) none of the above.

13. If a binary star is observed from directly above the orbit it cannot be detected as a spectroscopic binary. Why?
    A Its Doppler shift will be too large.   B) Stars emit no light at their poles.
    C) They will be eclipsing binaries instead.   D) Its parallax will be too small.
    E) No Doppler shift will be observed.

14. The luminosity of a star depends on
    A) its distance.   B) its Doppler shift.   C) its power output.
    D) both A) and B).   E) none of the above

15. A very luminous blue star is most likely to be which spectral class?
    A) A2   B) F2   C) O9   D) M4   E) G2

16. The faintest stars that can be seen in the sky with the unaided eye have a magnitude of 2.
    A) True   B) False

17. A star which is very luminous but cool must
    A) be very massive.   B) have a very large diameter.   C) be very distant.
    D) have a dim companion.   E) none of the above.

18. A star is the same radius of the Sun but is twice as hot. It must therefore be _____ as luminous.
    A) twice   B) four times   C) half   D) eight times   E) 16 times

19. A star has a parallax of 0.04 seconds of arc. Its distance is therefore
    A) 4 parsecs.   B) 4 light years.   C) 2.5 parsecs.   D) 0.25 parsecs.   E) 25 parsecs.

20. A star has a surface temperature twice that of the Sun's and a luminosity 10,000 times the Sun's. How big is its radius compared with the Sun's?
    A) 500.   B) 50,000.   C) 25.   D) 2.5   E) 250.

21. Two stars orbit each other with a period of a 1/10th year. They are 1/2 AU apart.
    What is their combined mass in solar mass units?
    A) 80   B) 0.8   C) 1.25   D) 12.5   E) none of the above.

In the HR diagram sketched at right, where will

22. variable stars be found?
23. white dwarfs lie?
24. red giants lie?
25. high-mass stars be on the main sequence?

```
  + A
   +           B   C
    +
     +
      +
       +
        +  E
       D   +
  _____
           Temp
```

26. Denote the surface temperature, radius, and luminosity of the Sun by T_o, R_o, and L_o respectively. If a star has $T=2T_o$, $R=3R_o$, its luminosity is _____ L_o.
    A) 6   B) 16   C) 36   D) 72   E) 144

27. A star has an observed parallax of 0.02 arc-sec. Its distance is _____ parsec.
    A) 0.02   B) 2   C) 20   D) 50   E) 500

28. One parsec is equal to about
    A) 1/3 light year.   B) 1 light year.   C) 3 light years.   D) 1018 cm.   E) 1018 km

29. Two stars are identical but are located at different distances. Star A is at 2 parsecs and star B is at 4 parsecs from the Earth. At the Earth the observed brightness of star B is seen to be _____ that of star A.
    A) 2 times   B) 1/2   C) 4 times   D) 1/4   E) 1/8

30. Star A has an apparent magnitude of 11, and star B has an apparent magnitude of 6. The observed brightness of star B is _____ times that of star A.
    A) 2.512   B) 5   C) 100   D) 1/5   E) 1/100

31. Among the spectral classes of stars, the coolest are
    A) A stars.   B) G stars.   C) K stars.   D) M stars.   E) O stars.

32. In O stars the optical lines of hydrogen do not show strong absorption because
    A) helium is more abundant than hydrogen.
    B) all of the hydrogen atoms are in the ground state.
    C) hydrogen is almost all ionized.
    D) O stars emit very little optical radiation.
    E) O stars are cool.

33. The absorption lines in a stellar spectrum provide information on
    A) the radial motion of the star.
    B) the surface composition of the star.
    C) the surface temperature of the star.
    D) all of the above.
    E) both B and C.

34. The two most abundant elements in stars, with the most abundant given first, are
    A) nitrogen, oxygen.   B) iron, hydrogen.   C) carbon, nitrogen.
    D) helium, oxygen.   E) hydrogen, helium.

35. In the H-R diagram, the main sequence extends from
    A) high luminosity, high temperature to low luminosity, low temperature.
    B) high luminosity, low temperature to low luminosity, high temperature.
    C) high luminosity, low temperature to low luminosity, low temperature.
    D) high luminosity, high temperature to low luminosity, high temperature.

36. The most fundamental of a star's properties is its
    A) luminosity.   B) temperature.   C) mass.   D) radius.   E) observed brightness.

37. For an eclipsing binary we observe the minimum amount of radiation from the system when
    A) the two stars are side by side as seen from the Earth.
    B) the hotter star is directly behind the cooler star.
    C) the hotter star is directly in front of the cooler star.
    D) the hotter star is moving towards us and the cooler star is moving away from us.
    E) None of the above statements is correct.

38. The hotter a star is, the more radiation it emits
    A) in shorter wavelengths.   B) in lower frequencies.   C) in higher frequencies.
    D) Both A and B are correct.   E) Both A and C are correct.

39. The surface temperature of the Sun is 5800 K, and the wavelength at which the Sun's emission peaks is 500 nm. If a star has a surface temperature four times that of the Sun, its emission will peak at a wavelength of _____ nm.
    A) 125   B) 250   C) 500   D) 1000   E) 2000

40. Two stars are identical but are located at different distances. Star A is at 8 parsecs and star B is at 4 parsecs. At the Earth the brightness of star B is seen to be _____ that of star A.
    A) 8 times   B) 4 times   C) 2 times   D) 1/2   E) 1/4

41. Denote the surface temperature, radius, and luminosity of the Sun by T_o, R_o, and L_o respectively. If a star has $T=2T_o$, $R=2R_o$, its luminosity is _____ L_o.
    A) 4   B) 16   C) 32   D) 64   E) 256

42. Which of the following is not a method used by astronomers to determine distances to stars?
    A) the parallax method.
    B) the luminosity-mass relation of main-sequence stars.
    C) the luminosity-temperature relation of main-sequence stars.
    D) the luminosity-period relation of Cepheid variables.

43. A star has an observed parallax of 0.05 arc-sec. Its distance is _____ parsecs.
    A) 0.05   B) 2   C) 5   D) 20   E) 50

44. Astronomers on Mars (1.5 AU. from Sun) would find the parallax (not the distance) of the nearest star to be
    A) the same as it is found to be from Earth.
    B) 50% larger than it is found to be from Earth.
    C) 50% smaller than it is found to be from Earth.
    D) unmeasurable.
    E) variable.

45. Binary stars provide astronomers with their primary method for measuring stellar
    A) luminosity.   B) mass.   C) chemical composition.   D) temperature.   E) radius.

46. Eclipsing binary stars provide astronomers with data not directly available from other binary systems The most important of these is the _____ of the stars.
    A) Temperature.   B) Luminosity.   C) Radius.   D) Mass.   E) Chemical Composition.

47. We see some binaries as spectroscopic and others as eclipsing systems. The quantity that makes them different is their
    A) orbital shapes.   B) orbital plane inclinations.   C) orbital velocities.
    D) orbital periods.   E) masses.

48. The majority of the known ECLIPSING binary stars have very short orbital periods. This is an example of a selection effect due to
    A) Kepler's third law.   B) Newton's second law.   C) the location of the Sun in the Milky Way.
    D) the uniformity of stellar masses.   E) the uniformity of nature.

49. The majority of the known VISUAL binary stars have very long orbital periods. This is an example of a selection effect due to
    A) Kepler's third law.   B) Newton's second law.   C) the location of the Sun in the Milky Way.
    D) the uniformity of stellar masses.   E) the uniformity of nature.

50. If the two eclipses of an eclipsing binary star result in EQUAL losses of light, then the two stars must have
    A) the same chemical compositions.   B) equal luminosities.   C) equal masses.
    D) equal temperatures.   E) equal sizes (radii).

51. The radius of each of the component stars of an eclipsing binary is determined by measuring the
    A) ratio of the amount of light lost in each eclipse.
    B) elapsed time between eclipses.
    C) duration time of each eclipse.
    D) wavelength of maximum intensity radiated by each star.
    E) orbital period.

52. Studies of binary stars reveal that the luminosities of main-sequence stars are determined entirely by their
    A) age.   B) mass.   C) temperature.   D) radius.   E) chemical composition.

53. Why are stars in a binary system often NOT perfectly spherical?
    A) One star heats the other.
    B) Magnetic forces of one star distorts the other.
    C) Their orbits may not be circles.
    D) One may have a larger pressure than the other.
    E) They may rises tides on each other.

54. Miss Cannon classified the spectra of the stars originally in order of increasing
    A) temperature.   B) complexity.   C) luminosity.   D) size.   E) apparent brightness.

55. Eventually Miss Cannon's spectral classes were rearranged in order of decreasing
    A) complexity.   B) temperature.   C) luminosity.   D) size.   E) brightness.

56. It is now realized that the significant differences in the appearances of Miss Cannon's spectral classes is due to differences in
    A) composition of the stars.   B) luminosity of the stars.   C) temperature of the stars.
    D) age of the stars.   E) all of the above.

57. When satellites discovered discrete X-ray sources in the sky, astronomers knew that could not come from ordinary stars because
    A) stars are too hot to emit much X-ray radiation.
    B) stars are not hot enough to emit much X-ray radiation.
    C) hydrogen cannot emit X-ray radiation.
    D) X-rays can only come from explosions.
    E) stars do not rotate fast enough to generate X-rays.

58. The principal reason for the differences of strength of the absorption lines of hydrogen in different stars is differences in the
    A) ages of the stars.
    B) amount of hydrogen in the stars.
    C) temperatures of the stars.
    D) diameters of the stars.
    E) luminosities of the stars.

59. The absorption lines of hydrogen are weak in the hottest stars because
    A) they have consumed most of their hydrogen.
    B) most of their hydrogen atoms are in the ground state.
    C) most of their hydrogen atoms have combined with helium atoms
    D) hot stars emit only ultraviolet radiation.
    E) most of their hydrogen atoms are ionized.

60. Astronomers on Earth find the distance to the nearest star to be 4 light-years. Astronomers on Jupiter (5 AU. from Sun) would find the distance to that star to be
    A) 4 light-years.   B) 20 light-years.   C) 0.8 light-years.   D) 0.3 light-years.   E) 12 light years.

In the HR diagram sketched below, identify the following important events in a low-mass star's lifetime.

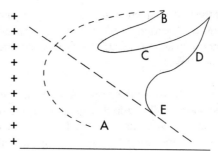

61. Stage of burning hydrogen
62. Stage of burning helium
63. Loss of a shell of gas
64. cessation of all nuclear burning
65. Expansion of its envelope

Chapter 12

1. White dwarfs form when
   A) a massive star explodes as a supernova.
   B) a low mass star's iron core collapses.
   C) a low mass star loses its outer layers as a planetary nebula.
   D) two red dwarf stars collide.
   E) a low mass star stops burning hydrogen.

2. When a star uses up its core hydrogen
   A) the core expands and cools.   B) the core shrinks and cools.
   C) the core shrinks and heats.   D) the core expands and heats.
   E) it just sits there inertly.

3. The radius of a white dwarf is about how large compared to the Sun?
   A) 10 times bigger.   B) 10 times smaller.   C) 100,000 times smaller.
   D) 100 times smaller.   E) They are about the same size.

4. What determines a star's lifetime?
   A) Its mass.   B) Its location in the galaxy.   C) Its luminosity.
   D) All of the above.   E) Only A) and C).

5. As a star moves off the main sequence, its core is_____and its envelope is _____.
   A) expanding, contracting.   B) expanding, expanding.
   C) contracting, expanding.   D) contracting, contracting.
   E) none of the above.

6. The reason that high-mass stars on the main sequence are more luminous than low-mass stars is related to
   A) high-mass stars needing a higher temperature to offset their higher gravitational compression.
   B) high-mass stars having more material which gives them a larger surface to radiate.
   C) high-mass stars are made of heavier elements which in turn gives them a bigger size.
   D) none of the above.
   E) The statement is backwards. Low-mass stars are more luminous.

7. When a massive star explodes as a supernova it leaves as a stellar remnant
   A) nothing.   B) a neutron star.   C) a white dwarf.
   D) a black hole.   E) only B) and D) are likely remnants.

8. If a star is in hydrostatic equilibrium
   A) it is in a stable binary orbit.
   B) it is generating energy at the same rate that the energy escapes
   C) it is near the end of its life and is expanding.
   D) it must be losing mass.
   E) its pressure and gravitational forces are in balance.

9. The conversion of hydrogen into helium in stars takes place by
   A) the carbon/nitrogen (CNO) cycle.   B) the triple alpha process.
   C) the proton-proton (p-p) chain.   D) all of the above.   E) only A) and C).

10. The shell of ejected gas around the remnants of some high mass stars is called a
    A) planetary nebula.   B) red giant bubble.   C) reflection nebula.
    D) excretion disk.   E) supernova remnant

11. The basic evolutionary sequence of a star like the Sun is
    A) red giant, protostar, white dwarf, planetary nebula, main sequence.
    B) protostar, planetary nebula, red giant, main sequence, white dwarf.
    C) main sequence, red giant, planetary nebula, white dwarf, protostar.
    D) protostar, main sequence, red giant, planetary nebula, white dwarf.
    E) protostar, red giant, blue supergiant, supernova.

12. A star like the Sun ceases to be a red giant when
    A) it blows up like a supernova.   B) it first begins to burn iron in its core.
    C) most of its core hydrogen is consumed.   D) when it finally forms a core of helium.
    E) it ejects its outer layers to form a planetary nebula.

13. Red giants get their name because they are
    A) very massive and composed of iron oxides which are red.
    B) very massive and of spectral class O.
    C) covered with huge prominences that glow with red light.
    D) very large in diameter and very hot.
    E) very large in diameter and very cool.

14. The Sun will end up eventually as a white dwarf.   A) True.   B) False.

15. Before becoming a white dwarf, a main sequence star will
    A) become a red giant and eject a planetary nebula.
    B) become a supernova. C) become a pulsar. D) all of the above.
    E) none of the above.

16. Which line shows the evolutionary track of a high mass star?

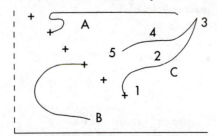

17. Along track C, which number corresponds to the ignition of helium?
    A) 1.   B) 2.   C) 3.   D) 4.   E) 5.

18. Interstellar reddening is caused by and is evidence for the existence in space of
    A) hydrogen gas.   B) 21 cm radiation.   C) dust grains.
    D) black holes.   E) the cosmic background radiation.

19. As the Sun ages it will
    A) become a red giant.
    B) become a white dwarf.
    C) become a planetary nebula.
    D) all of the above at some time or another
    E) None of the above.

20. A supernova explosion occurs when
    A) the core of a massive star begins to burn iron into uranium.
    B) the core of a massive star collapses in an attempt to ignite iron.
    C) a neutron star becomes a cepheid.
    D) tidal forces from one star in a binary tear the other apart.
    E) none of the above

21. A planetary nebula occurs when a
    A) low-mass stars experiences a helium flash.
    B) a high-mass star builds up a core of iron.   C) a high mass star collapses.
    D) a low-mass star builds up a core of carbon or oxygen and looses its outer layers.
    E) a protostar generates a bi-polar flow.

22. A planetary nebula is
    A) the disk from which the Solar System formed.
    B) another name for the rings of Saturn.
    C) the result of a supernova explosion.
    D) the source of comets.
    E) a shell of gas ejected from stars like the Sun near the end of their life.

23. Stars begin to evolve off the main sequence when
    A) their core begins to burn helium into carbon.
    B) the hydrogen in their core is nearly used up.
    C) their cores become iron.
    D) their cores become uranium.
    E) none of the above

24. High-mass stars live _____ than low-mass stars because _____.
   A) longer   they have more fuel to burn.
   B) less long they burn their fuel faster even though they have more fuel.
   C) less long nuclear reactions proceed more slowly in them.
   D) longer nuclear reaction proceed more slowly in them.
   E) none of the above make any sense.

25. Which track in the HR diagram is that of a star like the Sun?
   A) "Q"   B) "R"   C) "S"

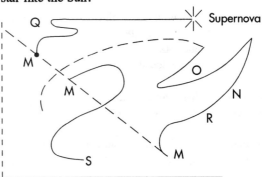

26. What fuel is burnt at the point "M" on the track labeled "Q"?
   A) hydrogen   B) helium   C) carbon   D) iron   E) none of the above

27. Is the fuel there burnt in A) the core? B) the envelope? C) a shell?

28. What fuel is burnt along the part of track "Q" labeled "N"?

29. What fuel is burnt at the point "M" on the track labeled "R"?
   A) hydrogen   B) helium   C) carbon   D) iron   E) none of the above

30. Is the fuel along the "N" part of the track burnt in
   A) the core?   B) the envelope?   C) a shell surrounding the core?

31. What fuel is burnt along the part of track "R" labeled "O"?
   A) hydrogen   B) helium   C) carbon   D) iron   E) none of the above

32. A white dwarf star is
   A) burning hydrogen.   B) burning iron.   C) burning helium.
   D) burning uranium.   E) simply cooling off.

33. The sketches below show the H-R diagrams of five star clusters. Which is the oldest cluster?
   A)   B)   C)   D)   E)

31. Which of the following statements about T-Tauri stars is incorrect?
    A) They are on their way to become main sequence stars.
    B) They often have surrounding disks.
    C) They often eject matter in two streams from their poles.
    D) All the above are true.
    E) None of the above are true.

32. Of the stages below describing the evolution of a star, the one a star spends the longest time in is
    A) the pre-main-sequence stage.
    B) the main-sequence stage.
    C) the post-main-sequence stage.

33. Stars within a cluster differ mostly in their
    A) distance.   B) mass.   C) age.   D) chemical composition.   E) All of the above.

34. The main sequence turn-off point is useful to determine a cluster's
    A) distance.   B) mass.   C) age.   D) chemical composition.   E) All of the above.

38. During the main sequence stage of a star, the property of the star that changes the most is
    A) its mass.   B) its radius.   C) its surface temperature.   D) its composition at the core.
    E) its composition at the surface.

39. From its position on the main sequence, a F star will
    A) move down along the main sequence to become a G star.
    B) move up along the main sequence to become an A star.
    C) become a red giant.
    D) move directly to the white dwarf region of the H-R diagram.
    E) stay on the main sequence indefinitely.

40. The more massive a star is
    A) the more luminous it is during its lifetime on the main sequence.
    B) the shorter will be its lifetime on the main sequence.
    C) the more likely it is to end up as a white dwarf.
    D) All of the above.
    E) Both A and B.

41. An important property of a Cepheid variable is the
    A) relation between its average luminosity and the period of its pulsation.
    B) relation between its average luminosity and its surface temperature.
    C) relation between its average luminosity and its mass.
    D) relation between its mass and its surface temperature.
    E) None of the above.

42. The relation between mass and luminosity for main sequence stars can be expressed roughly as $L = M^3$. An O star has a mass of 30 M_{Sun}. Its luminosity is _____ L_{Sun}.

    A) 2.7×10^4 B) 9×10^3 C) 2.7×10^3 D) 9×10^2 E) 27

43. In stars the gravitational force which tends to collapse a star is counterbalanced by
    A) rapid rotation.   B) electrical force in the atom.   C) magnetic force.
    D) thermal gas pressure.   E) nuclear force.

44. The C-N-O cycle is
   A) a process in which C, N, and O serve as catalysts in the fusion of 4 protons into a helium nucleus.
   B) a process in which oxygen is produced from nitrogen and carbon.
   C) a process in which carbon, nitrogen, and oxygen are produced from the fusion of helium nuclei.
   D) a process in which iron is produced from the fusion of carbon, nitrogen, and oxygen.
   E) a process in which neutrinos and oxygen (n and o) are emitted at the speed of light (c).

45. In order to begin nuclear fusion, a high temperature is required in the center of a star to overcome the
   A) electrical repulsion between protons.
   B) nuclear force between protons.
   C) nuclear force between neutrons.
   D) gravitational force between particles.
   E) pressure force due to particles.

46. The energy generated when 1 gm of hydrogen is transformed into helium nuclei is 6×10^{18} ergs gram^{-1}. If an A star radiates at a rate of $100 L_{Sun}$ ($1 L_{Sun} = 4 \times 10^{33}$ ergs sec^{-1}), it is transforming protons into helium nuclei at a rate of about
   A) 7×10^{14} gm per sec. B) 7×10^{16} gm per sec. C) 6×10^{18} gm per sec.
   D) 6×10^{20} gm per sec. E) 3×10^{25} gm per sec.

47. The above A star has $5 M_{Sun}$ ($1 M_{Sun} = 2 \times 10^{33}$ gm) of hydrogen. For 10% of all the hydrogen of the A star to be transformed into helium nuclei, the time it takes is about _____ years. (Note: 1 year = about 3×10^{7} seconds).
   A) 2×10^{7} B) 10^{8} C) 5×10^{8} D) 5×10^{9} E) 5×10^{10}

Chapter 13

1. What is the Chandrasekhar limit?
   A) The size of black hole.
   B) The maximum possible mass of a white dwarf.
   C) The distance from the center of the galaxy at which gas clouds turn into stars.
   D) The smallest mass a star can have and still burn hydrogen.
   E) None of the above.

2. A neutron star is
   A) the last stage in the life of a massive star.
   B) usually rotating extremely fast at its birth.
   C) a source of pulses of radio or light radiation.
   D) produced in a supernova explosion.
   E) all of the above.

3. Normal black holes are created by
   A) the collapse of stars like the Sun.   B) the collapse of high mass stars.
   C) relics left over from the early Universe.   D) the collision of red giants.
   E) the explosion of stars like the Sun.

4. Black holes are believed to form
   A) when a low mass star like the Sun ejects a planetary nebula.
   B) after a high mass star supernovas and its core collapses.
   C) when two stars approach one another and pass inside their Roche limit.
   D) when a star exhausts the hydrogen in its core.
   E) None of the above.

5. Neutron stars have diameters of about
   A) 1 AU.   B) 1 Solar Radius.   C) 1/100th Solar Radius.
   D) 100 miles.   E) 10 kilometers.

6. Elements heavier than iron are produced when a star
   A) is becoming a red giant.   B) is in its white dwarf stage.
   C) is a pulsar.   D) explodes as a supernova.   E) none of the above.

7. What is an accretion disk?
   A) Gas ejected during a planetary nebula event.
   B) Gas collected during a supernova explosion.
   C) Stars that collect around the galaxy's central bulge.
   D) Gas that accumulates around black holes and other compact stars.
   E) none of the above.

8. A type I supernova involves what type of star?
   A) T Tauri.   B) Cepheid.   C) O supergiant.
   D) white dwarf.   E) planetary nebula.

9. A white dwarf is about how much bigger (smaller) than the Earth?
   A) 10 times larger   B) 10 times smaller   C) 100 times bigger
   D) about the same size   E) 10,000 times smaller

10. If the Sun were to turn into a black hole
    A) we would immediately be dragged in.
    B) it would have a diameter of about 3 miles.
    C) it would bend the space in its vicinity.
    D) it would have a diameter of about 5000 miles.
    E) Only B) and C).

11. How do pulsars form?
    A) A massive star becomes a supernova and leaves behind a spinning neutron star core.
    B) A star like the Sun collapses as it tries to ignite helium in its core. The core picks up speed from burning material falling on to it which then flashes as the star spins.
    C) A white dwarf in binary star system exceeds the Chandrasekhar limit.
    D) A black hole exceeds the Schwarzschild limit and collapses.
    E) A white dwarf in a planetary nebula collapses and spins up.

12. How do black holes form?
    A) A star like the Sun collapses as its carbon core begins to fuse into oxygen.
    B) A white dwarf in a binary system explodes and the blast triggers the collapse of its companion.
    C) A Cepheid variable pulses too hard and gravity prevents its re-expansion.
    D) A massive star forms an iron core. When the core collapses and triggers a supernova blast, the core becomes a black hole if it is massive enough.
    E) All of the above can make black holes.

13. The radius of a solar mass black hole is about
    A) 10 meters. B) 100 meters. C) 0.1 meters. D) 3 meters. E) 3 kilometers.

14. Astronomers believe they have detected black holes from
    A) their Hawking radiation.
    B) x-rays emitted by hot gas orbiting around them.
    C) their silhouettes seen against bright background stars.
    D) the gamma rays they emit as they pulsate.
    E) the radio waves they emit as they spin.

15. A black hole is "black" because
    A) the escape velocity from its "surface" is the speed of light.
    B) it contains the iron from the core of its parent star, and the iron is so dense it blocks any light from escaping.
    C) it contains the iron from the core of its parent star, and the iron generates such a strong magnetic attraction on the light that none can escape.
    D) it is spinning so fast that its surface is moving faster than light.
    E) it has such a low mass that there is nothing there to generate light.

16. The pulses seen from a pulsar are caused by
    A) the star's radius expanding and contracting as it burns iron in its core.
    B) the star's rapid rotation sweeping beams of radiation across the viewer's line of sight.
    C) gobs of hot gas from an accretion disk falling rhythmically onto the star's surface.
    D) a dark companion periodically eclipsing the bright "pulsar" itself.
    E) None of the above.

17. If the Sun turned into a black hole but kept exactly the same mass it has now, the Earth would
    A) continue to orbit it as before, although the Sun would be dark.
    B) be rapidly pulled in.
    C) be tossed into a much larger and more elliptical orbit.
    D) be broken apart by the intense burst of gamma rays the black hole would emit.
    E) fly off into space as the black hole "sucked" in its own gravity.

18. If the mass of the collapsing core of a highly evolved star lies between about 1.4 and 3 M_{Sun}, this core will become
    A) a white dwarf.   B) a black dwarf.   C) a neutron star.   D) a black hole.

19. A neutron star is supported against gravity by
    A) neutron degeneracy pressure.
    B) fusion of neutrons.
    C) thermal gas pressure.
    D) electron degeneracy pressure.
    E) all of the above.

20. What would you expect the Sun will become eventually?
    A) An M star.   B) A white dwarf.   C) A supernova.
    D) A neutron star.   E) A black hole.

21. A pulsar is
    A) a pulsating K star.
    B) a pulsating white dwarf.
    C) a strongly magnetic, pulsating neutron star.
    D) a strongly magnetic, rotating white dwarf.
    E) a strongly magnetic, rotating neutron star.

22. Given that the Schwarzschild radius of a 3 M_{Sun} black hole is 9 km, the Schwarzschild radius of a 100 M_{Sun} black hole is
    A) 0.3 km.   B) 30 km.   C) 90 km.   D) 300 km.   E) 900 km.

23. The accretion of matter onto a white dwarf from a red giant in a binary system produces the phenomenon of
    A) nova.   B) supernova.   C) planetary nebula.   D) X-ray burster.   E) pulsar.

24. The largest mass a white dwarf can have is about
    A) 0.5 M_{Sun}.   B) 1.4 M_{Sun}.   C) 3 M_{Sun}.
    D) 10 M_{Sun}.   E) There is no limit to the mass.

25. Given that the Schwarzschild radius of a 3 M_{Sun} black hole is 9 km, can a photon at a distance of 15 km from a 6 M_{Sun} black hole escape?
    A) Yes.   B) No.

26. The size of a white dwarf is comparable to the size of
    A) the Sun.   B) the Earth.   C) the Earth's orbit.
    D) the State of Massachusetts.   E) Boston.

27. The demonstration in which the instructor stands on a spinning platform with arms extended aims to explain
    A) how a neutron star is spinning much faster than a main-sequence star or a white dwarf.
    B) how gravity can be balanced by rotation.
    C) how a fast-spinning object ejects matter into space.
    D) how the instructor can spin and talk at the same time.
    E) None of the above.

28. A neutron star is thought to be created by
   A) rapid accretion of interstellar gas.
   B) the collapse of the core of a dying massive star.
   C) coalescence of two stars in a close binary system.
   D) collision of two stars.
   E) none of the above.

Stars in General

1. Which of the following statements about the visible spectra of main-sequence stars is incorrect?
   A) In O stars the absorption lines of hydrogen are weak.
   B) The hotter stars appear bluer.
   C) G stars have a surface temperature of about 5000-6000 K.
   D) The spectra correlate with the stellar surface temperatures.
   E) All the above are true.

2. In the H-R diagram, the vertical and horizontal axes are respectively
   A) color and brightness.
   B) luminosity and mass.
   C) luminosity and temperature.
   D) spectral type and apparent magnitude.
   E) none of the above.

3. Which of the following statements about main-sequence stars is incorrect?
   A) They are supported against gravity by thermal gas pressure.
   B) They produce energy by the fusion of hydrogen into helium nuclei.
   C) There is a relation between the mass of the star and its luminosity.
   D) There is a relation between the luminosity of the star and its temperature.
   E) All of the above are true.

4. The protons and neutrons in a helium nucleus are bound together by the
   A) gravitational force.   B) electromagnetic force.   C) nuclear force.
   D) all of the above.,   E) none of the above.

5. Stars along the main sequence owe most of their differences to
   A) changing chemical abundances.
   B) their different masses.
   C) their different ages.
   D) their different radii.
   E) their apparent magnitudes.

6. The more massive a star is
   A) the shorter will be its lifetime on the main sequence.
   B) the hotter it will be during its lifetime on the main sequence.
   C) the more luminous it will be during its lifetime on the main sequence.
   D) All of the above.
   E) Both A and B.

7. Betelgeuse is a star that is intrinsically much more luminous than the Sun, yet has a surface temperature only about half that of the Sun. Betelgeuse must be a
   A) supernova.   B) nova.   C) red giant.   D) blue giant.   E) white dwarf.

8. Which of the following objects does not pulsate (i.e., expand and contract periodically in size)?
    A) A Cepheid variable.   B) An RR Lyrae variable.   C) The Crab pulsar.
    D) All of the above.   E) None of the above.

9. The evolution of white dwarf stars is primarily a process of
    A) continued contraction.
    B) collapse.
    C) spinning down to a slower rate.
    D) making heavy elements from carbon.
    E) cooling.

10. The ultimate source of the energy that the Sun and the stars radiate into the Universe is stored in the form of
    A) rotation.   B) magnetic fields.   C) radiation.   D) mass.   E) electric fields.

11. A star like our Sun owes its long stable life to its inefficient use of
    A) thermal radiation.   B) magnetic energy.   C) gravitational energy.
    D) nuclear energy.   E) rotational energy.

12. The radiation that comes to us from the surface of a star is most like that of a
    A) fluorescent light bulb.
    B) neon sign used for advertising.
    C) mercury vapor street lamp.
    D) filament of an incandescent light bulb.
    E) Bunsen burner gas flame.

13. When the Sun consumes most of the hydrogen in its core it will begin to
    A) explode.   B) expand.   C) contract.
    D) rotate faster. E) become hotter at the surface.

14. Carbon is much more abundant than gold (note the relative prices of coal and gold per pound). The reason is that
    A) carbon is made by the fusion of hydrogen.
    B) carbon is the principal energy source of the stars.
    C) gold is not a stable chemical element.
    D) carbon is needed for life, but gold is not.
    E) gold is formed only during supernova explosions.

15. The astronomer Kip Thorn described a star as a "glowing pause in the gravitational collapse of a cloud of gas." Which of the following contributes most to that "pause?"
    A) Rotation of the star.
    B) Fusion of hydrogen into helium.
    C) Neutrino pressure.
    D) Powerful magnetic fields.
    E) All of the above contribute during some part of a star's life.

16. When single stars vary significantly and periodically in brightness, the most likely cause is
    A) rotation.   B) pulsation.   C) explosion.   D) evolution.
    E) formation of dust grains in the photosphere.

17. Astronomers now think that pulsars are formed by
    A) the disintegration of binary stars.
    B) collapse of an accretion disk in binary stars.
    C) mass flowing between components of binary stars.
    D) explosions of stars called supernovas.
    E) disruption of white dwarf stars.

18. The repetitive explosions of novae are now thought to be caused by
    A) matter falling on to a white dwarf from a companion.
    B) collapse of the cores of massive stars.
    C) rapidly oscillating magnetic fields.
    D) extreme pulsational instability.
    E) rotation that exceeds the breakup limit.

19. Astronomers measure the distances to nearby stars by observing their
    A) brightness.   B) parallax.   C) speed.   D) proper motion.   E) apparent size.

20. Stars along the main sequence of the H-R diagram appear to have different amounts of hydrogen and other chemical elements in the spectrum of their light. This is actually caused by
    A) different amounts of hydrogen and other elements.
    B) different luminosities of those stars.
    C) different temperatures of those stars.
    D) absorption in our own atmosphere on the Earth.
    E) evolution of hydrogen into heavier elements.

21. Of all the physical properties of the stars, the one that is most nearly the SAME for all stars is
    A) luminosity.   B) radius.   C) chemical composition.
    D) surface temperature.   E) mass.

The next six questions refer to the stars indicated on the schematic H-R diagram sketched below.

22. Which of the stars is most like our Sun?
23. Which of the stars is a red giant?
24. Which of the stars is a white dwarf?
25. Which of the stars is the most common type that exists?
26. Which of the stars has the smallest size (radius)?
27. Which of the stars has the largest size (radius)?

```
| *E
|   *                            *D
|       *
|           *
|               *C
|                   *
|                       *
|           *A              *B
|
|_____
```

28. Astronomers are convinced that stars are evolving. What is the basis for that conviction?
    A) Stars have different masses.
    B) Stars all have the same chemical composition.
    C) Stars consume a finite fuel supply while releasing energy.
    D) Evolutionary processes have actually been observed.
    E) It is just a hypothesis with no convincing reasons.

29. Astronomers think that new stars are born in
    A) globular clusters.
    B) clouds of interstellar gas and dust.
    C) supernova explosions.
    D) binary star systems.
    E) giant elliptical galaxies.

30. The birth of a star is primarily a process of
    A) gravitational collapse.   B) nuclear reactions.   C) explosive nucleosynthesis.
    D) magnetic field interactions.   E) turbulent gas motions.

31. The Sun will die with most of its fuel supply unused because
   A) it is not rotating rapidly.
   B) it cannot mix its unburnt surface hydrogen into its core.
   C) its mass is so small.
   D) it will lose its mass.
   E) it is not hot enough to convert hydrogen to helium.

32. Most of the stars in our galaxy are now on the main sequence of the H-R diagram. That is because
   A) it is the only stable configuration for a star.
   B) most of the stars are very young.
   C) red giants only form from the most massive stars.
   D) it is the longest lived phase of stellar evolution.
   E) the galaxy is too young to have white dwarf stars.

33. Current theory indicates that our Sun will continue to be stable on the main sequence for another
   A) 1 billion years.   B) 5 billion years.   C) 10 billion years.   D) 100 billion years.
   E) an undeterminable but very long time.

34. Our knowledge of the interior structure of stars is based mainly on
   A) interpretations of the spectrum of starlight.
   B) computer models using current concepts of physics.
   C) the appearance of the H-R diagram.
   D) analysis of the orbits of binary stars.
   E) experiments with high energy atomic particles.

35. Astronomers think that the Sun will at the end of its lifetime become a
   A) supernova.   B) red giant.   C) black hole.   D) neutron star.   E) white dwarf.

36. A star like our Sun is stable because its powerful gravity is
   A) unable to compress hydrogen gas.
   B) balanced everywhere inside by gas pressure.
   C) balanced everywhere inside by radiation pressure.
   D) counteracted by nuclear reactions deep in its core.
   E) balanced by its rotation.

37. In order to be stable, a star like our Sun must
   A) rotate.   B) convert hydrogen to helium.   C) contract.
   D) expand.   E) radiate energy into space.

38. The Sun remains stable for a very long time because
   A) it is very large.
   B) it radiates like a black body.
   C) nuclear fusion replaces its radiated energy.
   D) it has a solid core.
   E) it has planets.

39. Astronomers do not ever expect to find a star 1000 times as massive as our Sun because
   A) the probability of such stars forming is very small.
   B) pressure from its radiation would prevent such a formation.
   C) there is not enough mass available to form such a star.
   D) such stars could only form in globular clusters.
   E) hydrogen fusion could not occur under such great pressure.

40. White dwarf stars are dead stars, but they continue to radiate energy because they
    A) convert helium to carbon.
    B) convert helium back to hydrogen.
    C) are cooling very slowly.
    D) contract slowly due to immense gravitation.
    E) reflect light from companion stars.

41. Which of the following does not provide a source of energy for a star's radiation during some part of its life?
    A) Fusion of hydrogen into helium
    B) Gravitational contraction.
    C) Fusion of helium into carbon.
    D) Fusion of carbon into magnesium.
    E) Magnetic pressure.

42. Many things that we use today, such as automobiles, are made from iron. What was the original source of the iron mined from the Earth?
    A) The Sun.
    B) The cores of an exploding supernovae.
    C) Mass lost from red giant stars.
    D) The nucleus of our own galaxy.
    E) The event that created the Universe.

43. If stars have been chemically EVOLVING by converting hydrogen into helium, why do they all appear to have the same chemical composition?
    A) They do not appear to have the same chemical composition.
    B) The conversion occurs only deep inside their cores.
    C) Interstellar hydrogen replenishes their supply.
    D) All stars are less than 6000 years old.
    E) Convection keeps the stars all homogenized.

44. Pulsars are currently thought to be
    A) rapidly rotating neutron stars.   B) pulsating neutron stars.   C) binary neutron stars.
    D) binary white dwarf stars.   E) pulsating white dwarf stars.

45. Why is evolution so seldom noticed in nature?
    A) Because it rarely occurs.
    B) It generally occurs on very long timescales.
    C) Scientists do not normally look for evolution.
    D) Evolution only happens to living things.
    E) Evolution causes only very subtle changes.

46. The first concept of stellar evolution was that stars evolve from
    A) hotter to cooler on the main sequence.
    B) cooler to hotter on the main sequence.
    C) larger to smaller on the main sequence.
    D) smaller to larger on the main sequence.
    E) none of the above.

47. Red giants are thought to be evolved stars rather than stars just being formed because
    A) stars are no longer being formed in our galaxy.
    B) we observe them to be expanding and not contracting.
    C) they have much more helium than main sequence stars.
    D) evolved red giants are stable far longer than protostars.
    E) they are much cooler than we expect protostars to be.

48. Theories of stellar evolution are tested observationally by
    A) observing how the Sun evolves.
    B) studying the surfaces of white dwarf stars.
    C) comparing components of close binary stars.
    D) determining the H-R diagrams of clusters of different ages.
    E) all of the above methods.

49. The age of a star cluster can be deduced from
    A) the number of stars it contains.
    B) the turn-off point of stars on its main-sequence.
    C) its location in the Milky Way galaxy.
    D) its radial velocity.
    E) its diameter.

Chapter 14
1. A Pop II star is
   A) red. B) blue. C) young. D) A) and C). E) B) and C).

2. What is the zone of avoidance?
   A) A region in the Solar System with no asteroids.
   B) The region of the sky where we can see few or no galaxies.
   C) A zone around massive black holes in which stars are disrupted.
   D) The zone that lies beyond the edge of the Universe.
   E) A region in the Earth through which earthquake waves can't travel.

3. Pop I stars formed
   A) during the Milky Way's initial collapse.
   B) after the main collapse and when gas accumulated in a disk.
   C) only during the last few thousand years.
   D) in the halo as gas is driven out of the nucleus.
   E) We don't know. There are no traces of Pop I stars today.

4. We believe the Milky Way is a spiral galaxy because
   A) we can see the spiral arms reflected in distant dust clouds.
   B) of the way the rotation velocity of the stars changes with distance from the center.
   C) radio observations of interstellar clouds show they lie in spiral arms.
   D) x-ray photographs show that red giants are bunched into a spiral pattern.
   E) none of the above are relevant.

5. Which is closest to the number of stars in the Milky Way?
   A) 100,000.   B) 10^8.   C) 10^{11}.   D) 10^{15}.   E) 10^{37}.

6. We can estimate how many stars there are in the Milky Way because
   A) we can count them, although it's very tedious.
   B) we can measure its mass from the Sun's motion and the modified form of Kepler's 3rd law. Dividing by the mass of an average star then gives the number of stars.
   C) aliens have told us.
   D) we can estimate how much it slows down neighboring galaxies.
   E) the color of the stars in the spiral arms when used with Wien's law, gives the number of stars.

7. In order to see a reflection nebula, the nebula must contain
   A) ionized hydrogen.   B) cold neutral hydrogen.   C) dust grains.
   D) interstellar molecules. E) ionized helium.

8. The light we see from emission nebula is created by
   A) ionized hydrogen.   B) cold neutral hydrogen.   C) dust grains.
   D) interstellar molecules. E) ionized helium.

9. An HII region is
   A) a zone of ionized hydrogen.   B) normally near hot young stars.
   C) likely to be found along a galaxy's spiral arms.   D) all of the above.
   E) Only A) and C).

10. In which part of the Milky Way are Pop I stars most likely to be found?
    A) Halo. B) Bulge. C) nucleus. D) disk. E) they are spread uniformly.

11. The amount of interstellar matter in the Milky Way is about how much compared to the stars?
    A) comparable to.   B) twice as much.   C) ten percent.
    D) 10 times as much.   E) 1000 times as much.

12. Population I stars in the Milky Way probably formed
    A) during the first stages of collapse of the galaxy.
    B) after most of the gas had collapsed into a rotating disk.
    C) after many supernova had enriched the interstellar medium with heavy elements.
    D) both B) and C)
    E) None of the above

13. A typical distance between stars near the Sun is about
    A) 100 AU.   B) 100 Light years.   C) a few million light years.
    D) a few billion light years.   E) a few light years.

14. What makes an HII region glow?
    A) Its slow gravitational collapse.
    B) It is heated by one or more hot O or B stars.
    C) It reflects starlight.
    D) The hydrogen in its gas is slowly undergoing cold fusion into helium.
    E) HII regions do not glow. They are dark.

15. One way we know where the Sun lies in the Milky Way is that
    A) we can see that the edges of the galaxy are equi-distant from us in all directions.
    B) radio signals from it are equally strong in all directions.
    C) globular clusters form a roughly spherical cloud and we lie off-center in it.
    D) all the stars near the Sun are moving away from us, implying we are near the core.
    E) stars near the Sun are moving parallel to the Sun, implying we are at the outer edge.

16. Which of the following statements about globular and galactic clusters is incorrect?
    A) They provide information about how stars evolve.
    B) Globular clusters are old while galactic clusters have a wide range of ages.
    C) Stars in globular clusters are metal rich while stars in galactic clusters are metal poor.
    D) Globular clusters are found in the halo of our Galaxy while galactic clusters are found in the disk.
    E) None of the above.

17. The evidence for the existence of an interstellar medium is provided by
    A) the ejection of matter from stars via supernova events, stellar winds, etc.
    B) the obscuration of light from distant stars.
    C) the presence of emission nebulae.
    D) the presence of O and B stars.
    E) all of the above.

18. Which of the following statements about the interstellar matter is incorrect?
    A) It is composed of a mixture of gas and small solid particles called dust grains.
    B) The gas in clouds near O and B stars is generally ionized.
    C) The gas in dense interstellar clouds is primarily molecular (i.e., H_2, H_2O, CO, etc.)
    D) The large interstellar clouds are the sites of star formation.
    E) All of the above are true.

19. Which of the following would you not expect to find in the halo of our Galaxy?
    A) K stars.   B) globular clusters.   C) O and B stars.
    D) white dwarfs.   E) None of the above.

20. Which of the following statements about our Galaxy is incorrect?
    A) It is a spiral galaxy.
    B) It consists of both a disk and a halo of stars.
    C) Stars form from the interstellar matter in the spiral arms.
    D) There is evidence, from how the speed of rotation of matter in the disk depends on its distance from the Galactic center, that there is a large amount of dark matter in our Galaxy.
    E) All of the above are true.

21. What is the approximate distance from the Sun to the galactic center in light years?
    A) 1,000   B) 8,000   C) 25,000   D) 100,000   E) 106

22. Herschel estimated the shape of our galaxy by
    A) looking for the bluest stars - objects he thought outlined its edge.
    B) counting the number of stars that lie in different directions.
    C) mapping out the dark dust clouds that he knew outlined the spiral arms.
    D) measuring the parallax of the globular clusters lying at the galaxy's edge.
    E) measuring the rotation speed of white dwarfs.

23. Shapley located the center of the Milky Way galaxy by measuring
    A) the distances to the most remote stars.
    B) the distances to the globular clusters.
    C) the velocities of the stars all around us.
    D) the velocities of the globular clusters.
    E) the amount of dust absorption in the disk.

24. About 90% of all the stars in the Universe are on the main sequence; but about 35% of the stars we see with our naked eye are red giants. This is an example of
    A) rapid stellar evolution.
    B) the inability of our eyes to see infrared wavelengths.
    C) a selection effect.
    D) the presence of interstellar dust near the Sun.
    E) the Sun being located in an unusual place in our galaxy.

25. Star counting in the disk of the Milky Way galaxy cannot be used to locate the center because
    A) the stars do not extend all the way to the center.
    B) there are too many stars to be counted.
    C) the stars are not uniformly distributed in the disk.
    D) interstellar dust obscures all but the nearest stars.
    E) stars are not confined to the disk.

26. Which of the following best reveals the spiral structure of the Milky Way?
    A) Globular clusters and their distribution.
    B) Interstellar dust.
    C) Radio emission from interstellar hydrogen.
    D) White dwarfs.
    E) Red giant stars.

27. In general, spiral structure is likely to occur in physical systems that have a disk shape and that
    A) rotate faster near the center than at the outer edge.
    B) rotate faster near the outer edge than at the center.
    C) rotate as a rigid structure.
    D) do not rotate.
    E) are expanding.

28. The spiral structure of our Milky Way galaxy is thought to be maintained by
    A) magnetic fields. B) density waves. C) rapid rotation.
    D) interaction of stars with interstellar gas. E) expansion of the galactic disk.

29. Our Sun moves on a nearly circular orbit around the Milky Way with a period of about
    A) 10 thousand years. B) 240 thousand years. C) 240 million years.
    D) 14 billion years. E) not possible to measure such a long period.

30. Star formation in the Milky Way is
    A) no longer taking place. B) occurring primarily in the spiral arms.
    C) occurring uniformly in the galactic disk. D) occurring only in globular clusters.
    E) occurring only in the inner nuclear region.

31. The youngest stars in the Milky Way are found
    A) in the globular clusters. B) in the halo of the galaxy. C) in the nucleus of the galaxy.
    D) in the disk of the galaxy. E) uniformly distributed everywhere in the galaxy.

32. The presence of interstellar dust in our galaxy caused Shapley to
    A) overestimate the size of the Milky Way.
    B) underestimate the size of the Milky Way.
    C) determine incorrectly the location of the Milky Way's core.
    D) argue that the Sun lies at the center of the galaxy.
    E) argue that the Sun lies at the very edge of the Milky Way.

33. If our galaxy were an ellipsoidal system rather than a spiral, how would the appearance of the night sky be different?
    A) Constellations would not exist.
    B) There would be no faint stars in the sky.
    C) The Milky Way band would not exist.
    D) There would be no red stars visible in the sky.
    E) There would be no appreciable difference.

34. The mass of the Milky Way galaxy is estimated by measuring
    A) the total number of stars detected.
    B) the velocity of the Sun in its orbit.
    C) the speeds of the stars within 100 parsecs of the Sun.
    D) the total amount of light detected.
    E) how fast it moves relative to nearby galaxies.

35. Astronomers cannot observe most of the stars in the Milky Way galaxy because
    A) most of them are too far away.
    B) there are no stars in the outer regions.
    C) the light has not yet reached us from the outer regions.
    D) interstellar dust obscures all but the nearest stars.
    E) we are not located at the center of the galaxy.

36. Our Sun is located in the disk of the Milky Way galaxy, about
    A) in the center.
    B) 8,500 parsecs from the center.
    C) 93 million miles from the center.
    D) in a region called the Large Magellanic Cloud.
    E) near the outermost edge of the galaxy.

37. Red dwarf and white dwarf stars together make up 90% of all stars in the Universe. However, when we look at the stars visible to the naked eye (9110 stars), we see NO red dwarfs or white dwarfs. This is an example of
    A) the inability of our eyes to see infrared wavelengths.
    B) astronomical incompetence.
    C) a selection effect.
    D) rapid stellar evolution.
    E) all of the above.

Chapter 15
1. Which type of galaxy contains the least amount of cold interstellar matter?
    A) Spiral.   B) Elliptical.   C) Irregular.

2. What is meant by dark matter?
    A) Mass that disappears into black holes.
    B) Mass made of anti-matter whose effect cancels out the gravity of ordinary matter.
    C) Mass that radiates strongly at radio wavelengths and is therefore invisible with ordinary light.
    D) Mass deduced to be present from its gravitational effect but which emits no visible light or other detectable radiation.
    E) None of the above.

3. Active galaxies such as Seyfert Galaxies are thought to be powered by
    A) gravitational lenses.   B) enormous black holes at their center.
    C) Numerous supernova explosions.   D) the formation of many low mass stars.
    E) The Big Bang.

4. Quasars
    A) are the most distant objects we can see.
    B) are abnormally luminous galaxies.   C) have huge redshifts.
    D) probably contain huge black holes.   E) All of the above.

5. A galaxy has a recession speed of 8,000 km/sec. If the Hubble constant is 50 km/sec/Mpc, how far away is the galaxy?
    A) Not enough information is given.   B) 400,000 light years.
    C) 40,000 megaparsecs.   D) 160 megaparsecs.   E) 16 megaparsecs.

6. Why do E type galaxies have so few young stars?
    A) They have little or no matter with which to make stars.
    B) They are too young to have begun star formation yet.
    C) All the young stars fall into their cores.
    D) Trick question. E galaxies actually have lots of young stars.
    E) None of the above.

7. Why do radio galaxies emit energy from outside their main body ?
    A) They leave a wake as they move through space.
    B) They attract matter which is heated when it gets just to their edges.
    C) They eject gas from an active core into the space outside them.
    D) The emission is an optical illusion caused by the galaxy's gravity.
    E) None of the above.

8. What is the Hubble Law?
    A) A relation between a galaxy's mass and radius.
    B) A rule that gives the spacing of the planets from the Sun.
    C) A relation between a galaxy's shape and gas content.
    D) A relation between a galaxy's distance and recession velocity.
    E) A relation between a galaxy's distance and size.

9. Why do we believe quasars are extremely luminous?
    A) We can see them at immense distances.
    B) They pulsate so regularly.
    C) They emit so much synchrotron radiation.
    D) They are so massive.   E) None of the above.

10. Radio galaxies are usually
    a) Spirals. B) Ellipticals. C) Irregulars. D) SO systems.

11. One reason we believe that active galaxies have tiny cores is that
    A) they change in brightness on short time scales.
    B) they are drawing in matter to their core.
    C) we see no radiation from their cores.
    D) All the above.
    E) None of the above.

12. Seyfert Galaxies are characterized by
    A) high mass halos. B) extremely bright spiral arms.
    C) small but very luminous nuclei. D) a nearly complete absence of Pop II stars.
    E) a nearly complete absence of Pop I stars.

13. The relative scarcity of pop I stars in Elliptical galaxies isn't surprising because
    A) they have so much interstellar matter that we can't see young stars in them.
    B) their rapid rotation makes it tough for new stars to form.
    C) their slow rotation causes newly formed stars to fall in to the center and be difficult to observe.
    D) they have so little interstellar matter for creating young stars.
    E) Ellipticals are actually mostly Pop I stars.

14. The name of the Milky Way's Galaxy cluster is
    A) the Magellanic cloud. B) the Hydra cluster. C) the primordial fireball.
    D) the Ursa Major cluster. E) the Local Group.

15. The galaxy cluster to which the Milky Way belongs is a rich cluster. A) True. B) False.

16. An object looking star-like has a very large redshift (100,000 km/sec) and its spectrum shows that it is ejecting hot gas. It is probably a
    A) Radio galaxy. B) dwarf irregular galaxy. C) Seyfert Galaxy.
    D) Quasar. E) A tidally disturbed galaxy.

17. Voids are
    A) a peculiar kind asteroid. B) hollow planetesimals.
    C) huge regions of space with few or no galaxies.
    D) holes in the Venusian cloud deck.
    E) regions in the centers of galaxies containing many black holes.

Match Galaxy description with type. Choices may be used more than once or not at all.
    A) Seyfert Galaxy. B) Quasar C) Tidally distorted galaxy D) SO galaxy
    18. Spiral galaxy with small, bright nucleus.
    19. Starlike object with surrounding fuzz, perhaps a jet too.
    20. Ring galaxy.

21. The radio waves produced by radio galaxies are created by
    A) 21 cm emission mechanism from HI.
    B) synchrotron emission of charged particles spiraling in a magnetic field.
    C) radiation from molecules such as CO spinning in cold clouds.
    D) neutrinos decaying into photons. E) none of the above.

22. The power source for active galaxies is believed to be
    A) the collapse of a massive star.   B) the supernova of an entire star cluster.
    C) magnetic energy created near a white hole.   D) a massive black hole.
    E) the emission of Hawking Radiation from a massive blue supergiant.

23. The velocity of a recession of a galaxy is 45,000 km/sec. If the Hubble constant is 100 km/sec/Mpc, what is the galaxy's distance?
    A) 4.5 Mpc.   B) 45 Mpc.   C) 450 Mpc.   D) 900 Mpc.   E) 450 pc.

24. A massive black hole at the center of some galaxies occurs because
    A) super-massive stars form there.
    B) a small (a few M_{Sun}) black hole forms there and subsequently grows by swallowing material from its surroundings.
    C) many small black holes created throughout the galaxy gradually sink toward the galaxy's core.
    D) it is formed as the galaxy collapses.   E) it is left over from the big bang.

25. The sort of galaxies found in a rich cluster are typically
    A) Spiral.   B) Elliptical.   C) Irregular.   D) Seyfert.   E) none of the above.

26. The Milky Way is what type of galaxy?
    A) Spiral.   B) Elliptical.   C) Irregular.   D) Ring.   E) Hubble.

27. The main physical difference between spiral galaxies and elliptical galaxies is that
    A) elliptical galaxies are always more massive than spiral galaxies.
    B) elliptical galaxies are always more luminous than spiral galaxies.
    C) elliptical galaxies consist mostly of old stars while spiral galaxies contain young luminous stars.
    D) elliptical galaxies are rotating faster than spiral galaxies.
    E) elliptical galaxies contain more dust than spiral galaxies.

28. The Hubble Law
    A) shows that the Universe is expanding.
    B) indicates that quasars are the most distant kind of objects observed.
    C) is a relation between recession velocity and distance of galaxies.
    D) All of the above.
    E) Both A and B.

29. If the distance of galaxy B is 4 times the distance of galaxy A, the velocity at which galaxy B is moving away from us is ____ times that of galaxy A.
    A) 16   B) 8   C) 4   D) 2   E) 1/4

30. Which of the following is not a property of quasars?
    A) They look brighter to us than any other objects in the night sky.
    B) They have much larger redshifts than galaxies.
    C) They are the most distant astronomical objects.
    D) They radiate strongly in the radio, optical, and X-ray wavelengths.
    E) Their active region is much smaller than the size of a galaxy.

31. The principal EVIDENCE that leads to the conclusion that all QUASARS are very distant from us is their
    A) very dim light.
    B) very large red-shifted spectrum.
    C) enormous output of energy.
    D) extremely small apparent size.
    E) variable output of light.

32. A strong piece of evidence that the active regions of quasars are very small is their
    A) very dim light.
    B) very large red-shifted spectrum.
    C) enormous output of energy.
    D) extremely small apparent size.
    E) variable output of light.

33. Many astronomers hypothesize that supermassive black holes exist at the centers of many galaxies. The EVIDENCE that prompts speculation is
    A) stellar explosions observed at the centers of galaxies.
    B) hydrogen gas concentrated at the centers of galaxies.
    C) high orbital speeds of stars near the centers of galaxies.
    D) large numbers of stars near the centers of galaxies.
    E) rings of gas observed near the centers of galaxies.

34. If most of the mass of a disk galaxy were concentrated in its central nuclear bulge, you would expect its outermost stars to
    A) all be very young.
    B) all be very old.
    C) escape.
    D) fall toward the center.
    E) rotate more slowly than the ones near the center.

35. Distances to the relatively nearby spiral galaxies are estimated by measuring
    A) the periods of their Cepheid variable stars.
    B) the brightness of supernovas that explode in their midst.
    C) the sizes of their star formation gas clouds.
    D) their apparent diameters.
    E) all of the above are useful distance indicators.

36. Evidence that the Universe contains much unobserved dark matter is the
    A) excessive amounts of gas found in spiral galaxies.
    B) fast rotation of spiral galaxies out to their edges.
    C) excessive amounts of dark dust in spiral galaxies.
    D) powerful radio emission from the centers of spirals.
    E) all of the above constitute evidence for missing mass.

37. Clusters of galaxies give evidence for unobserved dark matter by exhibiting
    A) large amounts of dark absorbing dust.
    B) far more ellipsoidal galaxies than spiral galaxies.
    C) large numbers of collisions among galaxies.
    D) powerful x-ray emission.
    E) velocities of their members that appear too fast for the cluster's mass.

38. Stars in the outermost regions of ellipsoidal galaxies move along paths so that they
    A) oscillate back and forth through the galaxy on elongated orbits.
    B) collect at the center.
    C) collide with other stars.
    D) escape on the other side.
    E) are torn apart by the strong tidal force.

39. Astronomers hypothesize that elliptical galaxies cannot form new stars to replace those that are evolving because
    A) they are spinning too rapidly to allow star formation.
    B) their tidal force disrupts star formation regions.
    C) they have so little cold interstellar gas and dust.
    D) they exist only in large clusters of galaxies.
    E) star formation requires rapid rotation.

40. Many clusters of galaxies contain a few gigantic elliptical galaxies among the thousands of smaller ones. A current theory contends that the giants are the result of
    A) excess gas and dust in the cluster.
    B) mergers of smaller galaxies.
    C) evolutionary expansion.
    D) weakening of the force of gravity.
    E) black holes in their central cores.

41. In nearby clusters of galaxies ellipticals are more numerous than spirals, but in remote clusters spirals appear to be more numerous. This supports the hypothesis that
    A) space is filled with absorbing intergalactic dust.
    B) spirals evolve into ellipticals.
    C) ellipticals evolve into spirals.
    D) there are strong observational selection effects at work.
    E) the Universe contains large amounts of dark matter.

42. Quasars all have very large red-shifts of their spectral lines. Astronomers think this indicates that quasars are
    A) ejected from other galaxies.
    B) very remote objects in the Universe.
    C) black holes erupting into the Universe.
    D) exploding.
    E) spinning.

43. If the red-shifts of the spectra of quasars are interpreted to mean they are at "cosmological" distances (that is, they lie at very large distances from us) then quasars must
    A) be emitting enormous amounts of energy from their cores.
    B) be exploding.
    C) be spinning at great speeds.
    D) be very old.
    E) not be made of ordinary matter (atoms).

44. The rapid variations of brightness observed in the light from some quasars is interpreted to mean that the light comes from
    A) highly ionized gas.   B) unobserved (missing) mass.
    C) very small volumes of material. D) very hot gas.   E) rapidly rotating gas.

45. When two galaxies collide with each other they are disrupted by
    A) collisions of their stars with each other.
    B) the gigantic explosion resulting from such a collision.
    C) the gravitational (tidal) forces that one exerts on the other.
    D) the very hot gases that are formed.
    E) the black holes in their cores.

46. Astronomers currently think that the radiation coming from quasars originates from
    A) a disk orbiting a supermassive black hole.
    B) dense accumulations of stars near the center of the quasar.
    C) collisions of stars near the center of the quasar.
    D) gas falling into the quasar from other galaxies.
    E) none of the above are currently favored theories.

47. Quasars are currently thought to be
    A) exploding galaxies.
    B) ordinary galaxies with very luminous nuclei.
    C) an illusion due to gravitational lensing.
    D) galaxies that are about to explode.
    E) objects made of an exotic unknown form of matter.

48. Many quasars have numerous absorption lines in their spectra that have many different red-shifts. Astronomers hypothesize that these lines are created by
    A) multiple explosions generating expanding gas clouds.
    B) changes in the structure of atoms as the quasar evolves.
    C) absorption by gas in galaxies between us and the quasars.
    D) shocks waves from multiple collisions.
    E) tidal effects from galaxies near the quasars.

49. Astronomers have recently discovered some pairs of quasars that appear close to each other and that have identical spectra. The current explanation for this is
    A) binary quasars in orbit around each other.
    B) gravitational lensing by an intervening galaxy.
    C) fission of one quasar into two quasars.
    D) a coincidence of accidental alignment.
    E) all of the above have been suggested as explanations.

50. Which of the following would be hardest to observe in any galaxy other than our own Milky Way?
    A) Cepheid variable stars.   B) Interstellar gas and dust.   C) Nova explosions.
    D) Supernova explosions.   E) White dwarf stars.

Chapter 16

1. How can we estimate when the Big Bang occurred?
   A) From the amount of iron in old stars.
   B) From the amount of uranium in terrestrial rocks.
   C) From the speed with which galaxies are separating.
   D) From the amount of iron in the Sun. E) None of the above.

2. The cosmic background radiation is
   A) light from very distant stars. B) an explanation of Olbers' Paradox.
   C) Energy emitted by black holes at the centers of nearby galaxies.
   D) Radiation from the birth of the Universe.
   E) Light from gravitational lenses.

3. An open universe is one that
   A) expands for ever.   B) expands to a maximum size and recollapses.
   C) contains huge amounts of mass and has a low expansion velocity.
   D) has an edge.   E) None of the above.

4. Which of the following is a resolution of Olbers' paradox?
   A) Dust blocks our view of distant stars.   B) Black holes absorb the light.
   C) The Universe has a finite age, so even if there is light from distant
      stars, it hasn't had time to reach us.
   D) Light disappears as it crosses space.   E) None of the above.

5. The expansion of the Universe proves that
   A) the Solar System is at its center.   B) the Universe is open.
   C) the Universe is closed.   D) the Universe was once pure iron.
   E) None of the above.

6. In the Inflationary Universe theory the Universe began with a radius about
   A) that of the Earth.   B) that of the Solar System.   C) that of a grapefruit.
   D) the size of a period.   E) far smaller than a proton.

7. The available <u>evidence</u> (not theory) at this time suggests the Universe is   A) open.   B) closed.

8. Astronomers believe that the Universe was created in a violent expansion of space and time because
   A) some distant galaxies have a blueshift, implying they were once extremely hot.
   B) a weak background radiation believed to be a relic of the explosion can be detected at radio wavelengths.
   C) large telescopes show a brightening in the sky at immense distances corresponding to very long ago.
   D) all of the above.
   E) Only A) and B)

9. The age of the Universe is close to
   A) 10 - 20 million years.   B) 10 - 20 billion years.   C) 10 - 20 thousand years.
   D) completely unknown.   E) none of the above are even close.

10. If the Universe is closed
    A) expansion continues forever.
    B) expansion eventually stops and the Universe collapses again.
    C) space will eventually become totally empty and dark.
    D) the expansion will slow, but never actually stop.
    E) none of the above.

11. The Big Bang refers to
    A) the creation of the Solar System.   B) the creation of the Moon.
    C) the origin of the heavy elements in a supernova.   D) the origin of the Universe.
    E) none of the above

12. Why is the cosmic background radiation so cool?
    A) It is emitted by cool stars.
    B) Interstellar dust absorbs and cools it.
    C) The expansion of the Universe has lengthened its wavelength, cooling it.
    D) It has emitted neutrinos which have cooled it.
    E) We are moving through it so fast it just looks cool.

13. We can detect the motion of the Earth through the cosmic background radiation because
    A) the radiation is slightly redshifted in one direction and blueshifted in the opposite direction.
    B) we receive a much stronger signal from the part of the sky we are heading toward.
    C) we receive a much weaker signal from the part of the sky we are heading toward.
    D) there are more galaxies visible in the direction we are heading.
    E) Trick question. We are at rest with respect to the radiation.

14. Olbers' paradox refers to
    A) the fact that the sky is dark at night
    B) the age of some stars seeming to be older than the Universe
    C) the creation of the Universe out of nothing
    D) the fact that some galaxies can be traveling away from us faster than light
    E) none of the above

15. The cosmic background radiation comes from
    A) Quasars   B) Radio Galaxies.   C) the Big Bang.
    D) the solar nebula.   E) none of the above.

16. The cosmic background radiation has a low temperature today because
    A) the Universe has expanded and expansion causes cooling.
    B) it is rich in heavy elements that absorb radiation very strongly.
    C) it was created with a low temperature.   D) it has gotten so far from the Sun.
    E) all the stars that were heating it have burnt out.

17. The age of the Universe can be deduced from
    A) the Hubble law.   B) Kepler's third law.   C) the Doppler shift law.
    D) the inverse square law.   E) Shapley's law.

18. The age of the Universe is about _____ years.
    A) 15 million.   B) 150 million   C) 1.5 billion   D) 15 billion   E) 150 billion.

19. The Universe seems to be open. To make it closed requires
    A) more mass.   B) less mass.   C) a higher rate of expansion.   D) both B) and C).
    E) older stars.

20. If an alien astronomer in a distant galaxy looks at the galaxies it can see, it will observe that
    A) other galaxies are moving toward it.
    B) other galaxies are stationary.
    C) other galaxies are moving away from it.
    D) half of the galaxies are moving away and half of them are moving toward it.
    E) other galaxies are rotating about it.

21. Most of the helium in our Galaxy is believed to be produced in
    A) the Big Bang. B) main-sequence stars. C) planetary nebulae.
    D) red giants. E) supernovas.

22. If the average density of the Universe were greater than the critical density, the Universe would
    A) eventually stop expanding and begin contraction.
    B) continue to expand forever.
    C) eventually stop contracting and begin expansion.
    D) continue to contract forever.
    E) expand and contract periodically about its present size.

23. Hubble's law of the redshifts is generally interpreted to mean
    A) the Universe is becoming cooler.
    B) galaxies are evolving.
    C) the Universe is expanding.
    D) the Universe is collapsing.
    E) the Universe is in a steady state.

24. The night sky is very dark, and astronomers regard that as EVIDENCE that
    A) the Sun has set.
    B) the Universe is not very large.
    C) the Universe is expanding.
    D) the Universe is not extremely old.
    E) distant galaxies have stopped emitting light radiation.

25. The (3 K) cosmic background radiation is now considered to be
    A) the remains of the original Big Bang creation radiation.
    B) evidence for cool gas between the galaxies.
    C) radiation from the most distant galaxies not yet seen.
    D) radiation from the dust in galaxies.
    E) a complete and total mystery with no known explanation.

26. Which of the following CANNOT be used to estimate the distance to any galaxy?
    A) The red-shift of its spectral lines.
    B) The Cepheid variables within the galaxy.
    C) White dwarf stars within the galaxy.
    D) Exploding supernovas within the galaxy.
    E) Clouds of ionized hydrogen gas within the galaxy.

27. Which of the following observed properties of the Universe is evidence that the Universe is NOT infinitely old?
    A) Red-shifts in the spectra of very distant galaxies.
    B) Galaxies exist only in clusters.
    C) Most of the observed mass of the Universe is hydrogen.
    D) The night sky is dark.
    E) Our Sun is still on the main sequence.

28. The kind of universe we live in is fundamentally determined by
    A) the sizes of the galaxies within the Universe.
    B) the physical extent of the Universe.
    C) the number of galaxies within the Universe.
    D) the density of all matter in the Universe.
    E) the temperature of the cosmic background radiation.

29. A major contemporary unsolved problem concerning the kind of universe in which we live is the nature of
    A) quasars.   B) black holes.   C) the unobserved dark matter.
    D) the cosmic background radiation.   E) peculiar active galaxies.

30. Vast numbers of galaxies lie relatively near to us (nearer than 1 billion light-years), but not even one quasar is that close. This fact is compelling evidence that
    A) the Universe is expanding.
    B) the Universe has evolved.
    C) the Universe is in a steady state.
    D) redshifts cannot be Doppler shifts.
    E) galaxies formed very recently.

31. The darkness of the night sky is regarded as EVIDENCE that
    A) the Universe is expanding.
    B) the Universe is filled with absorbing dust.
    C) our own galaxy has a finite boundary.
    D) red-shifts do not give valid measures of expansion.
    E) galaxies have been radiating for only a finite time.

32. Current cosmology asserts that the Universe came from a single creation event about 15 billion years ago. Evidence for this is
    A) the Hubble law of the red-shifts.   B) the cosmic background radiation.
    C) the darkness of the night sky.   D) the uniformity of the abundance of hydrogen and helium.
    E) all of the above.

33. According to the General theory of Relativity, the force of gravity results from
    A) pressure exerted by light radiation.
    B) curvature of spacetime.
    C) interatomic forces.
    D) magnetic fields.
    E) the expansion of the Universe.

34. If the geometry of the Universe is closed, then the Universe
    A) must evolve.   B) must expand.   C) will eventually collapse.
    D) is in a steady state.   E) must be rotating.

35. Astronomers recently discovered that the cosmic background radiation temperature has very small fluctuations all over the sky. Some astronomers take this as evidence that
    A) the original universe was not perfectly uniform in density.
    B) galaxies absorb some of the cosmic background radiation.
    C) there never was a "Big Bang" creation event.
    D) there are great voids in space between the galaxies.
    E) there are patches of absorbing dust in the Universe.

36. Direct observational evidence that the scale of the Universe is expanding is shown by the
    A) cosmic background radiation.
    B) darkness of the night sky.
    C) red-shifts of the spectra of distant galaxies.
    D) existence of quasars.
    E) clustering of the distant galaxies.

37. Which of the following correct statements is evidence that evolution has occurred in the Universe?
    A) Distant galaxies appear smaller than nearby galaxies.
    B) Distant galaxies appear dimmer than nearby galaxies.
    C) Ellipsoidal galaxies do not contain gas or dust.
    D) All quasars are very distant from us.
    E) Ellipsoidal galaxies outnumber spiral galaxies.

GENERAL QUESTIONS FOR FINALS

1. Why do astronomers think that dark matter exists?
    A) They see gaps in the asteroid belt.
    B) The masses of galaxies found from Kepler's law disagree with masses deduced from the visible starlight they emit.
    C) It is the only explanation of the huge black holes found in some galaxies.
    D) There are too many neutrinos seen from outer space.
    E) They sky looks dark at night and something must block the light.

2. If you looked at a cepheid, an RR Lyra star, or a T Tauri star you would note
    A) that they are clumped into tiny groups.
    B) they are among the hottest stars known.
    C) that they are always binary stars.
    D) that their light output varies with time.
    E) none of the above

Match the following types of phenomena with their description
    3. Roche Limit   A) distance at which tidal forces cause breakup
    4. Doppler shift   B) relation between color and temperature
    5. Hubble law   C) relation between galaxy distance and velocity
    6. Kepler's 3rd law   D) relation between velocity and wavelength
    7. Wien's Law   E) relation between orbital period and size

8. You notice a small group of stars some clear winter night. With a pair of binoculars you see that there are several dozen of them in a loose irregular group. You must be looking at
    A) the Milky Way.   B) a globular star cluster.   C) an open star cluster.
    D) the Local Group. E) a meteor shower.

9. Why does the Moon rise about an hour later each night?
    A) Because of precession.   B) Because of the Earth's orbital motion around the Sun.
    C) Because the Moon's orbit is elliptical.
    D) Because the Moon moves in its orbit around the Earth.
    E) Because the Earth's rotation axis is tilted.

10. The Sun generates energy <u>now</u> by
    A) burning hydrogen into helium.   B) Helium into carbon.   C) silicon into iron.
    D) gravitational contraction and compression.   E) None of the above.

11. Which will burn out faster   A) the Sun or   B) a blue supergiant?

12. Astronomers believe that there must be "dark matter" because
    A) the outer parts of galaxies rotate more rapidly than can be accounted for by their observed mass.
    B) galaxies in clusters seem to move faster than they should given the cluster masses that are observed.
    C) material that falls into black holes must go somewhere..
    D) the Universe seems to be expanding too fast for its mass.
    E) all the above except C).

13. If the Sun shrank from its present radius to 1/100th its present size and its mass remained the same, its density would be
    A) decreased by a factor of 100.   B) increased by a factor of 100.   C) increased by a factor of 300.
    D) increased by a factor of 1 million.   E) Its density wouldn't change.

14. If the Sun shrank from its present radius to 1/4th its present size and its mass remained the same, its rotational speed would   A) increase.   B) decrease.   C) be unaffected.

15. This result (question above) occurs because of
    A) Wien's law.   B) Conservation of angular momentum.   C) Kepler's third law.
    D) Newton's third law.   E) The Doppler shift law.

16. Where in the Universe are heavy elements currently being made?
    A) Inside black holes.
    B) In interstellar dust and gas clouds.
    C) In the surface layers of low-mass stars.
    D) In the cores of massive stars.
    E) No heavy elements are currently being formed. They all formed in the Big Bang.

17. How did the planets form?
    A) They were captured by the Sun as it passed through a gas cloud.
    B) They are debris from a companion star that used to orbit the Sun and that blew up as a supernova.
    C) They were ejected from the Sun as clots of hot gas during intense solar flares.
    D) They were created during the Big Bang.
    E) They formed from dust grains that orbited the Sun in its youth and which stuck together to form progressively larger objects.

18. In the nuclear reaction $p + p \longrightarrow {}^2H + e^+ + \nu$, the nucleus ${}^2H$ contains
    A) 1 proton and 1 neutron.
    B) 1 proton and 2 neutrons.
    C) 2 protons and 1 neutron.
    D) 2 protons.
    E) 2 neutrons.

19. The measurements of radial motions of astronomical objects have been instrumental in
    A) the discovery that our Universe is expanding.
    B) mapping the rotation of our Galaxy.
    C) determining the masses of stars in a binary system.
    D) All of the above.
    E) None of the above.

20. The Sun's age is closest to
    A) 5 million years.   B) 50 million years.   C) 500 million years.
    D) 5 billion years.   E) 5 trillion years.

21. Among the stars, the densest is
    A) an O star.   B) a white dwarf.   C) a neutron star.
    D) a Cepheid variable.   E) a red giant.

22. If one were to look down at the Earth from above the north pole, the Earth would be spinning
    A) clockwise.   B) counter-clockwise.

23. The Sun is not a first generation star because
    A) it contains significant amounts of heavy elements in its surface layers.
    B) our galaxy is not a first generation galaxy.
    C) first generation stars are more massive than the Sun.
    D) first generation stars are hotter than the Sun.
    E) None of the above.

24. Most of the carbon, nitrogen, oxygen, and other heavy elements on the Earth were originally produced in
   A) the Big Bang.   B) our Sun.   C) the formation of the Earth.
   D) massive stars that have evolved.   E) interstellar clouds.

The following list contains five observed facts (DATA). Questions 1 - 4 consist of statements about the Universe. For each, identify which fact (A-E) constitutes EVIDENCE that supports the statement.

   A) The visible stars appear to be uniformly distributed all over the night sky.

   B) Most known globular clusters are in the direction of the constellation of Sagittarius.

   C) The spectral lines of all distant galaxies are shifted to long (red) wavelengths.

   D) Virtually all O and B stars are found in or near gas and dust clouds.

   E) Essentially no external galaxies are observed in the plane of the Milky Way in the night sky.

25. The Sun is NOT at the center of our Milky Way galaxy.
26. The Universe is expanding.
27. Stars form within interstellar clouds.
28. The disk of our Milky Way contains much dust.

29. Each of the following statements is correct, but only one is EVIDENCE that evolution has occurred in the Universe. Which one is evidence for evolution?
   A) Very distant galaxies appear smaller than nearby ones.
   B) Very distant galaxies appear dimmer than nearby ones.
   C) Ellipsoidal galaxies contain no free gas and dust.
   D) Quasars are only found very far away.
   E) There are more ellipsoidal galaxies than spiral galaxies.

PUTTING IT ALL TOGETHER - FINAL QUESTIONS
A WALK UNDER THE NIGHT SKY

You have learned much about the sky and the things that happen which can be seen. The real significance of any knowledge is the ability to apply it in reality. Imagine that you are walking with a friend just after the Sun has set, while a nearly full Moon is low in the southeastern sky. Your friend asks

30. Why we always see the same face of the Moon. You reply that it is because
   A) the Moon does not rotate on an axis.
   B) the rotation period of the Moon equals its orbital period.
   C) all sides of the Moon look alike.
   D) the Sun never illuminates the other side.
   E) the other side is seen by the other hemisphere of Earth.

31. Your friend remarks that the Moon is "full" tonight, but you tell him (or her) that it is not full yet, and you know that because
   A) it is too low in the southeastern sky.
   B) it is not yet perfectly round.
   C) it rose before sunset.
   D) it rose after sunset.
   E) it cannot be full if it is not in eclipse.

32. Seeing the bright planets Venus, Jupiter, and Saturn aligned from the western sky, you show your friend that the line connecting them with the Moon is very nearly
   A) the celestial equator.
   B) the Greenwich meridian.
   C) the Milky Way.
   D) the Zenith.
   E) the ecliptic.

33. Your friend asks how you can tell the planets from the stars and you reply that the definitive test for a planet is that it
    A) is brighter than all of the stars.
    B) moves relative to the stars.
    C) never twinkles as stars do.
    D) does not rise or set as stars do.
    E) has color whereas stars are all white.

34. "Can the Moon ever get in front of a planet?", your friend asks, and you tell him (or her) that it can do so but only very rarely because
    A) the orbit of the Moon is an ellipse.
    B) the planets are so much farther away than the Moon.
    C) planets have retrograde motions but the Moon does not.
    D) the orbit of the Moon is tilted 5 degrees from the ecliptic.
    E) the Moon moves much faster than the planets move.

Now that you have finished a course in astronomy, you could take a friend outside on some dark, clear night and explain to him (or her) some remarkable things that are known about stars. For example,
you could point out that stars have different colors and show your friend examples of orange colored stars and blue colored stars (even though you do not know their names).

35. You would then tell your friend that the different colors are caused by
    A) different chemicals present in the star's atmospheres.
    B) Doppler shifts caused by their motions.
    C) different surface temperatures.
    D) different luminosities.
    E) dust in space that absorbs light.

36. You would then show your friend an example of a cool star by pointing to one that is
    A) bright.   B) blue.   C) orange.   D) dim.   E) twinkling rapidly.

37. "Of all the stars we can see in the sky this moment, which is the largest one?" your friend asks. You search the sky and then point to one that is
    A) bright and blue.   B) bright and red.   C) twinkling very rapidly.
    D) brighter than all other stars.   E) moving faster than all other stars.

38. Your friend asks if it is possible that the stars shine by just reflecting sunlight, the way that our Moon and planets do. You reply that this is certainly not true, and we know that because
    A) stars appear to have different colors.
    B) stars generally have different absorption lines than our Sun has.
    C) stars twinkle, and the Sun does not.
    D) stars are not large enough to reflect enough sunlight.
    E) the Sun does not shine at night.

39. Your friend asks if you know what the stars are made of, and you reply that they are all made mostly of
    A) carbon and oxygen.
    B) hydrogen and oxygen.
    C) carbon and nitrogen.
    D) hydrogen and helium.
    E) fire.

40. Having taken a geology course, your friend says that the Earth is made of mostly iron and silicon, and he (she) wonders why the Earth is so different from the stars. This, you say, is a result of
    A) nuclear fusion of the Earth's hydrogen into iron.
    B) burning of all the Earth's hydrogen to make water.
    C) stars being so hot that they melt all their iron.
    D) the manner in which the Earth formed.
    E) the Earth being hit by meteors full of iron and silicon.

41. You surprise your friend by pointing out that most of the visible stars are very distant, and the nearest ones cannot be seen with eyes alone because most stars in the Universe are
    A) large and hot.   B) small and hot.   C) small and cool.
    D) large and cool.   E) dead and hence not radiating any light.

42. "Are the brightest stars the nearest ones to us?" your friend asks, and you say they are not necessarily close because
    A) brightness of stars does not depend upon distance.
    B) big stars must always appear brighter than small stars.
    C) bright stars have much more hydrogen than dim stars.
    D) some are binary stars that emit twice as much light.
    E) even a distant star may look bright to us if it emits vastly more energy than the Sun.

As you walk home at the end of a delightful evening of star gazing, your friend asks you the name of a bright orange star nearly overhead. You do not know its name, or even if it has one, but you recognize that it must be a distant red giant, far larger than our Sun. You have come to know the stars in a vastly more meaningful way than by the arbitrary names given to them by primitive people who lived long ago and who knew nothing about what the stars really are!

43. You tell your friend that our Sun is one of many stars in a gigantic stellar system shaped like a disk, and you provide evidence for that by pointing to
    A) bright red stars.   B) bright blue stars.   C) the Milky Way.
    D) the north star.   E) the horizon.

44. If you wanted to point out a very young star to your friend, you would point to one that is
    A) bright.   B) blue.   C) red.   D) dim.   E) double.

45. Your friend asks how you can tell that a star is young just by looking at it, and you explain that because the star is _____ it must be young.
    A) bright it must be nearby and we know that the stars nearby and therefore
    B) blue it is probably very bright and therefore consumes its fuel faster than our Sun so
    C) red it has not had a chance to start burning its fuel and so
    D) dim it is still heating up and so
    E) double it has not yet merged like our Sun did and therefore

46. Your friend wonders just what the age of such a young star might be, and you reply that its age is roughly
    A) a few thousand years.
    B) a few hundred thousand years.
    C) several million years.
    D) hundreds of millions of years.
    E) billions of years.

47. You might then show your friend an example of an evolved star by pointing to one that is
    A) bright.   B) blue.   C) red.   D) dim.   E) double.

48. Your friend is amazed that you can tell such a fact just by looking at a star without knowing its name. You explain that any such stars that are not evolved would be
    A) in clusters.   B) too dim to see with the naked eye.   C) non-existent.
    D) double.   E) moving away from us so fast we would have difficulty seeing them.

49. Your friend wonders what the fate of such an evolved star will be, and you tell him that it might become a
    A) supernova.   B) neutron star.   C) black hole.   D) white dwarf.   E) Any of the above.

50. Your friend asks what keeps the stars glowing, and you reply that they are releasing energy by
    A) slowly contracting under their own gravity.
    B) converting hydrogen to helium.
    C) burning carbon like a log in a fireplace.
    D) burning hydrogen to make water.
    E) converting helium to carbon.

51. You point out to your friend that all stars must eventually die and cease to glow because
    A) they are leaking their mass out into space.
    B) they will all explode.
    C) they will consume all their core hydrogen.
    D) all hot things cool down.
    E) they will collide with other stars.

52. "Can we see any dead stars tonight?", your friend asks, and you reply that
    A) all the blue stars are really dead stars.
    B) no stars have died yet in this galaxy.
    C) dead stars do not radiate any light.
    D) astronomers cannot tell which stars are dead.
    E) all dead stars are too faint to be seen with eyes alone.

53. Suddenly a bright light streaks across the sky, and your friend calls it a "falling or shooting star". You tell him that is a poor name to describe a
    A) comet crossing the sky.
    B) tiny meteoric particle vaporizing in our atmosphere.
    C) strange form of heat lightening.
    D) black hole evaporating.
    E) small piece of a star that broke away.

54. Your friend wonders how large the Milky Way is and you tell him that its diameter is about
    A) 1000 light years.   B) 8000 light years.
    C) 80,000 light years.   D) one million light years.   E) ten million light years.

55. Your friend notices that the Milky Way looks clumpy rather than uniform. He asks why this is so and you tell him that it is caused by
    A) non-uniformity of the disk of stars.
    B) star formation being random and haphazard.
    C) rotation of the Milky Way galaxy.
    D) nearby clouds of interstellar absorbing dust.
    E) tidal action of the distant galaxies.

56. Your clever friend says, "if we are inside a disk of stars, then why do we see stars all over the sky instead of only in the Milky Way?" You think for a moment and then realize this is evidence that
   A) most stars are not really in the Milky Way galaxy.
   B) most visible stars are really very nearby to us.
   C) interstellar dust must be very far away.
   D) the Sun is in a very unusual location in the galaxy.
   E) we are very near to the center of the Milky Way galaxy.

57. "Are we near the center of the Milky Way disk of stars?" your friend asks, and you inform him that we are
   A) almost exactly in the center of the great galaxy disk.
   B) out on the edge of the disk.
   C) about 28,000 light years from the center of the disk.
   D) far outside of the disk.
   E) over 1 million light years from the center of the disk.

58. Your friend sees that the Milky Way surrounds us completely, so he wonders how astronomers figured out where we are in the disk. You point toward the center and inform him that
   A) most red giant stars are in that direction.
   B) most young stars are in that direction.
   C) most of the interstellar dust is seen there.
   D) most supernovas occur in that direction.
   E) most globular clusters are in that direction.

59. "How many other stars besides our Sun are in the Milky Way galaxy?" your friend asks, and you reply that there are about
   A) 100 million stars.   B) few billion stars.   C) few hundred billion stars.
   D) few hundred trillion stars.   E) countless billions and billions.

60. "How could astronomers possibly have counted such a large number?" your friend wonders, and you point out that
   A) astronomers can count higher than anyone else.
   B) it is just a very crude guess.
   C) the Sun's orbital speed reveals how much mass is present.
   D) stars in other galaxies can be counted easily.
   E) it is the total amount of light that is measured.

61. "Is the Milky Way the edge of the Universe?" your friend asks, and you reply that it is not the edge, but that the Universe is made up of
   A) billions of other galaxies much like our own.
   B) billions of globular clusters.
   C) stars and gas surrounding our Milky Way extending far out.
   D) vast numbers of black holes.
   E) atomic particles.

62. "How far away do the astronomers think the galaxies extend?" asks your friend, and you reply that they probably extend to
   A) about 15 million light years.   B) about 150 million light years.   C) about 1.5 billion light years.
   D) at least 15 billion light years.   E) more than 150 billion light years.

63. "What keeps them from all falling together?" your friend asks, and you reply that they would do that except that they are all
   A) receding from each other at great speed.   B) evolving.   C) colliding with each other.
   D) rotating.   E) aging.

64. "What is the evidence for that belief?" your friend inquires and you tell him that the light from the farthest galaxies
   A) moves much slower than light from the nearby stars.
   B) is very much dimmer than it should be for their distance.
   C) is shifted to longer wavelengths, implying the galaxies are moving away from each one another.
   D) takes a long time to reach the Earth, implying that their light has not yet had time to turn around.
   E) has not yet reached the Earth.

65. "If the Universe is so big, why are we not blinded by all the light from so many distant galaxies whose number compensates their distance"? You reply that they would, but
   A) intergalactic dust absorbs the light from the remote ones.
   B) the expansion of the Universe weakens the remote ones.
   C) there are not enough galaxies to light up the night sky.
   D) the Universe is not old enough to have filled up with light.
   E) light from the most remote galaxies has not gotten here yet.

66. Your friend asks, finally, if the Universe will ever stop expanding, and you tell him that
   A) it must stop some day.
   B) it cannot possibly stop expanding ever.
   C) astronomers still do not know the answer to that mystery.
   D) we can never know the answer to that mystery.
   E) "God made Hell for people who ask questions like that." (a quote from St. Augustine)

OBSERVATIONS OF PLANETS AND MOON

1. When the planet Saturn is seen in the southern sky shortly after sunset, then Saturn would be nearly in
   A) superior conjunction.   B) inferior conjunction.   C) retrograde.
   D) eastern quadrature.   E) western quadrature.

2. If the planet Jupiter is seen close to a full Moon in the sky, then Jupiter must be in
   A) superior conjunction.   B) inferior conjunction.   C) retrograde.
   D) eastern quadrature.   E) western quadrature.

3. The constellations seen in each of our seasons are different. This happens because
   A) the Earth rotates upon its axis.
   B) the Earth orbits the Sun.
   C) the Earth is round.
   D) the Earth precesses.
   E) the stars are more distant than the Sun.

4. The full Moon will be seen highest in the sky when the Sun is nearly on the
   A) summer solstice.   B) winter solstice.   C) vernal equinox.
   D) autumnal equinox.   E) ecliptic.

5. Farmers refer to the full Moon as the "harvest Moon" when the full Moon rises at nearly the same time each evening. This can only occur when the Sun is nearly on the
   A) summer solstice.   B) winter solstice.   C) vernal equinox.
   D) autumnal equinox.   E) ecliptic.

6. If the planet Mars is reported to be in opposition, you would expect
    A) to see it rising shortly before sunrise.
    B) to see it setting shortly after sunset.
    C) to see it close to a first quarter Moon.
    D) to see it in retrograde.
    E) not to be able to see it at night.

7. When the Moon is in eastern quadrature, it is usually referred to as being
    A) new. B) first quarter. C) full. D) third quarter. E) the Moon cannot ever be in quadrature.

8. One month from now a constellation that we see overhead at 9:00 P.M. tonight will be seen at 9:00 P.M. to be
    A) nearly overhead.   B) lower in the western sky.   C) lower in the eastern sky.
    D) lower in the southern sky.   E) already set below the western horizon.

Answer Key

Introduction

1. A
2. A
3. B
4. C
5. B

Chapter 1

1. A
2. C
3. C
4. B
5. D
6. A
7. B
8. E
9. E
10. D
11. B
12. A
13. E
14. C
15. D
16. B
17. E
18. A
19. C
20. A
21. B
22. D
23. D
24. D
25. D
26. B
27. D
28. E
29. D
30. E
31. D
32. C
33. B
34. B
35. B
36. D
37. C
38. B
39. B
40. E
41. B

Chapter 1 cont'd

42. E
43. A
44. D
45. E
46. B
47. A
48. E
49. A
50. E
51. E
52. B
53. D
54. D
55. B

Essay 1

1. B
2. A
3. A

Chapter 2

1. A
2. D
3. D
4. A
5. D
6. D
7. C
8. B
9. E
10. E
11. C
12. C
13. A
14. D
15. C
16. B
17. D
18. A
19. A
20. E
21. B
22. A

Chapter 3

1. B

Chapter 3 cont'd

2. B
3. B
4. C
5. E
6. B
7. A
8. B
9. C
10. B
11. A
12. B
13. D
14. A
15. D
16. B
17. B
18. D
19. E
20. A
21. E
22. E
23. D
24. C
25. C
26. B
27. D
28. B
29. D
30. A
31. B
32. B
33. A
34. B
35. A
36. A
37. E
38. A
39. D
40. D

Essay 2

1. C

Chapter 4

1. E
2. D
3. D

Chapter 4 cont'd

4. B
5. D
6. C
7. E
8. C
9. D
10. C
11. C
12. C
13. E
14. C
15. D
16. C
17. D
18. A
19. D
20. D
21. C
22. D
23. E
24. E
25. E

Chapter 5

1. C
2. C
3. E
4. E
5. C
6. C
7. B
8. A
9. E
10. A
11. A
12. E
13. C
14. C
15. B
16. A
17. E
18. D
19. A
20. E
21. B
22. D
23. A
24. A
25. D

Chapter 5 cont'd

26. B
27. D
28. B
29. D
30. A
31. B
32. C
33. E
34. A
35. C
36. E
37. C
38. C
39. C
40. A
41. B
42. E
43. B
44. C
45. C
46. C
47. C

Essay 4

1. C
2. E
3. D
4. D
5. E

Chapter 6

1. C
2. C
3. D
4. A
5. C
6. D
7. D
8. D
9. D
10. D
11. E

Chapter 6 cont'd	Chapter 8 cont'd	Solar System--General cont'd	Chapter 10 cont'd	Chapter 11 cont'd
12. D	21. D		12. B	28. C
13. E	22. A	28. A	13. B	29. D
14. B	23. B	29. A	14. B	30. C
15. E	24. C	30. C	15. C	31. D
	25. E	31. E	16. E	32. C
Chapter 7	26. D	32. E	17. D	33. D
	27. E	33. D	18. A	34. E
1. E	28. D	34. C	19. D	35. A
2. C	29. C	35. A	20. A	36. C
3. A	30. E	36. C	21. A	37. B
4. D	31. D	37. C	22. C	38. E
5. A	32. B	38. C	23. E	39. A
6. D	33. E	39. A	24. A	40. B
7. D	34. E	40. A	25. B	41. D
8. B	35. E	41. B	26. C	42. B
9. D	36. D	42. A	27. E	43. D
10. D	37. A	43. C	28. E	44. B
11. C	38. A	44. A	29. D	45. B
12. B	39. E	45. A	30. D	46. C
13. E	40. A	46. A	31. A	47. B
14. C		47. A	32. D	48. A
15. A				49. A
16. C	Solar System--General	Chapter 9	Chapter 11	50. D
17. D				51. C
18. E		1. D	1. A	52. B
19. A	1. D	2. E	2. D	53. E
20. E	2. C	3. C	3. E	54. B
21. E	3. B	4. B	4. C	55. B
22. C	4. B	5. A	5. B	56. C
23. B	5. B	6. A	6. A	57. B
	6. E	7. E	7. C	58. C
Chapter 8	7. C	8. A	8. B	59. E
1. D	8. A	9. E	9. C	60. A
2. E	9. E	10. C	10. E	61. E
3. D	10. B	11. E	11. D	62. C
4. A	11. B	12. B	12. A	63. B
5. E	12. A	13. B	13. E	64. A
6. E	13. B	14. A	14. C	65. D
7. C	14. A		15. C	
8. A	15. E	Chapter 10	16. B	Chapter 12
9. D	16. C		17. B	
10. A	17. D	1. C	18. E	1. C
11. E	18. E	2. D	19. E	2. C
12. B	19. A	3. B	20. C	3. D
13. D	20. C	4. E	21. D	4. E
14. B	21. E	5. D	22. B	5. C
15. E	22. B	6. A	23. D	6. A
16. E	23. C	7. C	24. C	7. E
17. D	24. D	8. C	25. A	8. E
18. A	25. A	9. E	26. E	9. E
19. B	26. D	10. D	27. D	10. E
20. C	27. C	11. D		11. D

Chapter 12 cont'd

12. E
13. E
14. A
15. A
16. A
17. C
18. C
19. D
20. B
21. D
22. E
23. B
24. B
25. B
26. A
27. A
28. A
29. A
30. C
31. B
32. E
33. D
34. D
35. B
36. B
37. C
38. D
39. C
40. E
41. A
42. A
43. D
44. A
45. A
46. B
47. C

Chapter 13

1. B
2. E
3. B
4. B
5. E
6. D
7. D
8. D
9. D
10. E
11. A
12. D

Chapter 13 cont'd

13. E
14. B
15. A
16. B
17. A
18. C
19. A
20. B
21. E
22. D
23. A
24. B
25. B
26. B
27. A
28. B

Stars in General

1. E
2. C
3. E
4. C
5. B
6. D
7. C
8. C
9. E
10. D
11. D
12. D
13. C
14. E
15. B
16. B
17. D
18. A
19. B
20. C
21. C
22. C
23. D
24. A
25. B
26. A
27. D
28. C
29. B
30. A
31. B
32. D

Stars in General cont'd

33. B
34. B
35. E
36. B
37. B
38. C
39. B
40. C
41. E
42. B
43. B
44. A
45. B
46. A
47. D
48. D
49. B

Chapter 14

1. A
2. B
3. B
4. C
5. C
6. B
7. C
8. A
9. D
10. D
11. C
12. D
13. E
14. B
15. C
16. C
17. E
18. E
19. C
20. E
21. C
22. B
23. B
24. C
25. D
26. C
27. A
28. B
29. C
30. B
31. D

Chapter 14 cont'd

32. A
33. C
34. B
35. D
36. B
37. C

Chapter 15

1. B
2. D
3. B
4. E
5. D
6. A
7. C
8. D
9. A
10. B
11. A
12. C
13. D
14. E
15. B
16. D
17. C
18. A
19. B
20. C
21. B
22. D
23. C
24. B
25. B
26. A
27. C
28. D
29. C
30. A
31. B
32. E
33. C
34. E
35. A
36. B
37. E
38. A
39. C
40. B
41. B
42. B

Chapter 15 cont'd

43. A
44. C
45. C
46. A
47. B
48. C
49. B
50. E

Chapter 16

1. C
2. D
3. A
4. C
5. E
6. E
7. A
8. B
9. B
10. B
11. D
12. C
13. A
14. A
15. C
16. A
17. A
18. D
19. A
20. C
21. A
22. A
23. C
24. D
25. A
26. C
27. D
28. D
29. C
30. B
31. E
32. E
33. B
34. C
35. A
36. C
37. D

General Questions for Finals

1. B
2. D
3. A
4. D
5. C
6. E
7. B
8. C
9. D
10. A
11. B
12. E
13. D
14. A
15. B
16. D
17. E
18. A
19. D
20. D
21. C
22. B
23. A
24. D
25. B
26. D
27. D
28. E
29. D
30. B
31. B
32. E
33. B
34. D
35. C
36. C
37. B
38. B
39. D
40. D
41. C
42. E
43. C
44. B
45. B
46. C
47. C
48. B
49. E
50. B

General Questions for Finals cont'd

51. C
52. E
53. B
54. C
55. D
56. B
57. C
58. E
59. C
60. C
61. A
62. D
63. A
64. C
65. D
66. C

Observations of Planets and Moon

1. D
2. C
3. B
4. B
5. D
6. D
7. B
8. B